ARCHITECTURE
A SPOTTER'S GUIDE

CLASSICAL TEMPLES TO
SOARING SKYSCRAPERS

ARCHITECTURE
A SPOTTER'S GUIDE

CLASSICAL TEMPLES TO
SOARING SKYSCRAPERS

EDITORS

Sarah Cunliffe
Sara Hunt
Jean Loussier

METRO BOOKS
NEW YORK

EDITORS
Sarah Cunliffe, Sara Hunt, Jean Loussier

CONTRIBUTORS
Sarah Cunliffe, Clare Haworth-Maden, Sara Hunt, Michael Kerrigan,
Donna F. Shelmerdine, Stephen Small, and M. Jane Taylor.

Metro Books
122 Fifth Avenue
New York, NY 10011

ISBN 13: 978-1-4351-2436-3

Printed and bound in China

1 3 5 7 9 10 8 6 4 2

Page 2: From the Victorian to the Modernist era:
the clash of urban styles is what makes our cities distinctive.

ACKNOWLEDGMENTS

The publisher would like to thank Deborah White, Robin Langley Sommer, Sara Myers, Jennifer June, Wolfgang Kaehler, and Balthazar Korab, as well as all those whose photographs appear in this volume.

All photographs are © 2005 or 2010 **JupiterImages** unless otherwise listed here. Grateful acknowledgment is made to the following individuals and institutions for permission to reproduce illustrations and photographs:

© **Adagio** 60 b; © **Doris Antony** 225 t; © **Atlant** 69 t; **Bauhaus-Archiv** 228; © **James Armitage** 35 b; © **Thierry Bézecourt** 187 b; © **Jim F Bleak** 258 b; © **Marco Bonavoglia** 83 t; © **Manfred Brückels** 225 b; © **Massimo Catarinella** 37 l; © **Chachu207** 87 t; **Corel** 164, 170; © **Alessio Damato** 88; © **Andrew Dunn** 267; © **Ecelan** 45 r; © **Endo Shuhei Architect Institute** 269 all; **Raphael Azevedo Franca** 56 t; © **Andy Gilham** 43 t; © **Gisling** 55 both; © **Gryffindor** 214; © **Sara Hunt** 143 b, 213 b, 215 b, 257 c; © **663Highland** 56; © **Rudi Holnsteiner** 116, 161 b, 183 t; © **Georges Jansoone** 81 b; © **Wolfgang Kaehler** 12, 25 b, 26 b, 28, 30, 38, 45 all, 46, 47 b, 48, 49 all, 51 b, 78, 95 tr, 104, 108, 110, 135, 208, 216, 240, 249, 257, 260; © **KaTeznik** 43 b; © **A.F. Kersting** 192 all, 193; © **Balthazar Korab** 2, 11 b, 15 t, 111 t, 124, 125, 136, 149, 151, 154, 163, 165 b, 168, 174, 175, 179 t, 180, 181 t, 182, 185 b,188, 194, 200, 201 t, 203 b, 204 t, 207 t, 209b, 210, 211 b, 222, 224, 233, 238, 239 all, 241, 246, 251–53 all, 262; © **Hui Lan** 271 b; **Library and Archives Canada** 120 t; **Library of Congress, Historic American Buildings Survey** 109 (HABS NM,25-SANFE,2-6) M. James Slack, 111 b (HABS CAL,37-SANDI, 1-3) Henry F. Withey, 115 t (HABS CONN,2-FARM,9-3) Robert Fulton, 118 (HABS ME,3-SAB,2-1) Miller/Swift Photogra-phers, 119 (HABS NH,7-CANT,43) Bill Finney, 123 t (HABS VA,37-NUT.V, 1-5) Jet Lowe, 127 t (HABS GA,61-ATLA,20-1) Martin Stupich, 143 all (HABS ARIZ,10-TUCSON.V,3-5 and HABS ARIZ,10-TUCSON.V,3-20) John P. O'Neill and Donald W. Dickensheets, 160 (HABS DC,WASH,520B-128) Jack E. Boucher, 167 r (HABS CAL,12-EUR,6-2) Jack E. Boucher, 169 (HABS RI,3-NEWP,36-2) Jack E. Boucher, 172 (HABS RI,1-BRIST,18-1) Cervin Robinson, 173 (HABS RI,3-NEWP,44-1) Jack E. Boucher, 177 b (HABS NY,11-HUD,1-4) Cervin Robinson, 178 t (HABS MD,2-ANNA,65/1-10) John T. Lowe, 184 (HABS CONN,2-HARF,16-10) Robert Fulton, 201 b (HABS MO,96-SALU,49-32) Paul Piaget, 203 t (HABS ILL,16-CHIG,60-7), 204 b (HABS IOWA,97-SIOCI,3-3) Jack E. Boucher, 206 (HABS ORE,3-GOCA.V,1-4) Marvin Rand, 208 t (HABS CAL,19-LOSAN,65-8) Marvin Rand, 229 (HABS MASS,9-LIN,16-2) Jack E. Boucher, 231 t (HABS CAL,30 NEWBE,1-1) Marvin Rand, 236 l (HABS NY,31-NEYO,151-1) George Eisenman; **Library of Congress, Historic American Engineering Record** 209 t (HAER MONT,45-THOFA,3A-5) Lon Johnson, 230 (HAER PA,65-NEKEN,3-2) Jet Lowe, 231 b (HAER PA,65-NEKEN,3B-2) Jet Lowe, 264 t (HAER NY,31-NEYO,165-4) Jack E. Boucher; **Library of Congress, Prints and Photographs Division** 31, 68, 69 all, 70 l, 72 t, 73, 75 all, 83 b, 123 b, 126, 127 b, 128, 132, 141 b, 143c, 144, 148, 156, 183 b, 185 tr, 191 all, 197 tl & tr, 218, 219 all; © **Vincent Lostanlen** 97 tl; © **Magnus Manske** 90–91, 257 t; © **Nikki Fesak McKenna** 44, 62, 66, 67 t; © **McPolu** 69 b; © **Nepenthesi** 265; © **Jaume Ollé** 42 r; © **Ozeye** 90 t; © **Pahu** 258 t; © **Picabu** 211; © **Dennis Rausch** 60 t; © **Reynolds Plantation**, Greensboro, Georgia 185 tl; © **Paul Rocheleau** 205, 226, 227, 232, 237; © **Saraband Image Library** 10 t, 33 t, 36 b, 47 t, 76, 77 t & bl, 93 t, 139 b, 147, 150 l, 178 b, 179 b, 198–99 all, 212 b, 214; © **Simon Saunders** 8, 11; © **Doug Sim** 35 c; © **Taj Images** 208 t; © **Teach46** 34; © **Tony Tiger** 268; © **Tumbleweed Tiny House Company** 260 t; © **Urban** 35 t, 89; © **Väsk** 255 b; © **Davide Cesare Veniani** 42 l; © **Richard Wasenegger** 255 t; © **Wiii** 261 b; © **Wing** 249.

CONTENTS

INTRODUCTION

Architecture reflects the priorities, technology, artistic imagination, aspirations, faith, and power structures of the culture in which it is found. Frank Lloyd Wright called it the mother of all the arts. Whatever your viewpoint, the built environment cannot be ignored and will always be a talking point, at the very least; perhaps even a passion. Traveling opens our eyes to architecture, for it is usually only when we switch into tourist mode that we really take the time to look at the buildings that surround us. And while the sheer antiquity, monumentality, or beauty of certain constructions— such as Egypt's pyramids, India's Taj Mahal, or Indonesia's Borobudur—arouse such awe that they become tourist hot spots in themselves, most guidebooks urge travelers to visit a notable cathedral, skyscraper, palace, temple, or castle to learn more about the people who created it and what inspired them.

OPPOSITE: *The Classical building elements of column and lintel, and later, arch and dome, provided foundations for architecture that have endured for more than two thousand years. The styles and proportions used by the ancients, too, have been revived and reinterpreted, rejected and rebelled against, over the millennia.*

MONUMENTS TO THE PAST

The story of architecture is also the story of humankind's ingenuity and inventiveness. We look in wonder upon the pyramids of Giza, in the ancient city of Memphis (now part of Cairo, Egypt), and try to imagine how they could have been constructed more than four-and-a-half millennia ago. The largest monument, the Great Pyramid of Cheops, consists of more than 2 million blocks of stone, each of which weighs 2 tons or so. But before these great structures (perhaps mausoleums or observatories?) were assembled, people of many different cultures had found creative solutions to their needs for shelter and public space. Many prehistoric and ancient indigenous styles have proved impermanent, however, which is why we have concentrated on permanent structures from the Classical era onward in this book.

Top: *Carvings and plaques on medieval European buildings sometimes indicated the use (or owner's occupation) of the building they adorned.*

A Guidebook with a Difference

Architecture: A Spotter's Guide is far more than a travel guide, however, partly on account of its sweeping global and historical scope, and partly because it does not restrict itself to "important" edifices, but also embraces humbler homes, civic buildings, offices, and commercial structures—the bedrock buildings upon which societies are built. Learn more about these constructions through the history and language of architecture, and you will learn more about the civilizations that raised and used them, about their lives and times, and about what they feared and worshipped, despised and prized.

An On-the-Spot Informer

This is an on-the-spot guide, a book to be slipped into a pocket, which is why it is a comprehensive introduction to the world's major architectural trends and traditions, not an exhaustive history or gazetteer. Being a spotter's guide, it also focuses on the building types and styles that readers are most likely to encounter on their travels. Note that although some of these can often appear remarkably similar, wherever they may be seen in the world (bungalows are common in the United States, England, and India, for instance, while Australians are as familiar with the "shotgun" house as Americans), style names may vary by country, and that not all styles can be neatly compartmentalized and categorized. Where space allows, readers are alerted to alternative names and terminologies, as well as to overlaps with other styles.

Learn About Your Locality

Finally, if you have bought this book as a vacation guide, why not also take it with you when you're out and about in your own neighborhood? Do some architecture spotting close to home, and you may deepen your knowledge of your community, and perhaps ultimately even of yourself, for as Sir Winston Churchill sagely noted in *Time* magazine, "We shape our buildings: thereafter they shape us" (September 12, 1960).

ABOVE: *Old collides with new in a busy London street.*
BELOW: *Shanghai, China, is a showcase of new architecture.*

THE
CLASSICAL
HERITAGE

Variations on the Classical styles of architecture that were developed during the first millennium BC are so widespread that it is hard to walk through any city in the Western world without confronting many examples. Classically inspired columns, pediments, domes, and arches dominate a significant proportion of our public buildings, while even modest family homes frequently display doorways, windows, porches, and other details that borrow from Classical models.

OPPOSITE: *The Temple of Bel (Zeus, or Jupiter), in Palmyra, Syria, was built on the site of a shrine dating back to the second millennium BC. The temple was dedicated in AD 32.*

THE CLASSICAL STYLE

Influences from Earlier Civilizations

It is hard to believe that such influence has been exerted by a 2,500-year-old civilization of small city-states that were scattered around the eastern Mediterranean. But when the Greeks crystalized the architectural traditions of their ancestors in the region, as well as their Persian and Egyptian neighbors, they laid down foundations for Western architecture that are still intact.

Columns and Lintels

In the sixth century BC, the ancient Greeks perfected the use of columns and lintels (vertical supports bearing the weight of horizontal beams) to create structures of unparalleled clarity, symmetry, and power. This Classical style is best symbolized by the elegant Doric and Ionic temples of the fifth century BC. The purity and beauty of buildings such as the Parthenon and the Erechtheion on the Acropolis in Athens, Greece, had a profound influence on later architects, and especially on the Romans.

The Greek Influence on Later Architecture

As their empire expanded across the Mediterranean world in the first and second centuries BC, the Romans used Greek styles (and Greek architects) to build imposing, practical, and technically brilliant buildings. But the Romans did not merely imitate. They developed new materials (notably concrete), built on a grander scale, and added curves—the arch, vault, and dome—to the straight lines of the post-and-lintel architecture that had been perfected by the Greeks.

STYLE FILE

Notable Features:
Common elements in all the Classical styles include symmetry and visual order, as well as the use of columns that supported lintels, arches, and vaults.

Where and When:
Mediterranean region; c. 6th century BC to 3rd century AD.

BELOW: *Columns that supported load-bearing lintels were among the basic components of Classical architecture. These columns are from the temple of Ercole in Agrigento, on the isle of Sicily, southern Italy.*

LEFT: *The U.S. Capitol Building in Washington, DC, displays Classical features including its Roman dome and arches and graceful Corinthian columns. It was built in 1793 to a design by William Thornton and subsequently modified by Neoclassicist Benjamin Henry Latrobe.*

THE CARYATID

Columns were occasionally replaced by caryatids in some temples. These larger-than-life-sized female figures, standing on bases and bearing the entablature on heads adorned with richly carved capitals, lend a gracious human element to some elegant temples. A fine example is the south porch of the Erechtheion on the Acropolis.

Grand Ambitions

The Romans also set about building a much wider range of public structures. As well as temples and theatres, they married Classical styles with engineering prowess to create aqueducts, bridges, palaces, basilicas, bath houses, and sewers—many of which still stand today. In doing so, the Romans gave to posterity a rich architectural vocabulary that we have returned to repeatedly whenever we have sought symmetry, order, and beauty in our built landscape.

THE CLASSICAL ORDERS

The Classical orders of Doric, Ionic, and Corinthian are three styles of post and lintel that have been used and developed by architects from Classical times to the present day. Together with the Roman dome and arch, they are the basic vocabulary of most architecture in the Western, Classical tradition.

What Is an Order?

An order defines the style and structure of the columns, capitals, and entablature used in a building. How the column is fluted; what style of decoration the capital has; the structure and ornamentation of the frieze and cornice—all of this is set by rules.

The principal sections of an order are the column (which has a capital on top and, depending on the order, a base below) and the entablature (which typically consists of an architrave, a frieze above that, and then a layer of stone jutting out above the frieze, which is called a cornice).

THE ENTABLATURE

The entablature consists of a cornice (A), frieze (B), and architrave (C), as shown in the diagram below.

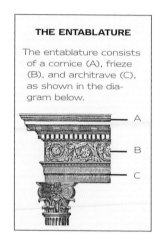

BELOW: *The triumphal Arch of Titus, Rome, is of Composite order.*

How Orders Were Used

Some buildings, like the Parthenon, follow a single order (i.e., Doric). But many Classical buildings combine orders, such as the Propylaea on the Acropolis, which combines Doric and Ionic, and the Temple of Apollo at Bassae, Greece, which has a Doric exterior, an Ionic interior, and the first known example of a Corinthian column inside.

The Romans often combined orders. The exterior of the Coliseum, for example, stacks Doric, Ionic, and Corinthian floors on top of each other. Eventually, new orders developed, using and modifying features of the original models, such as the Tuscan, Roman Doric, and Composite, which mixed elements of the Corinthian and Ionic orders.

THE DORIC ORDER

The first, and simplest, order to develop was the Doric—appearing between about 1000 and 600 BC. It was perfected in the late sixth and early fifth centuries BC. Its roots in earlier architectural styles are clear. Some elements are reminiscences of the structural necessities of wooden construction petrified in stone as ornamental features.

Simple Supports

The plain, fluted Doric columns emerge directly from the plinth (there is no column base). The fluting may have evolved from tied bundles of reeds or sticks, placed into holes in the ground, that were used for supports in earlier times.

The plain, circular echinus (an inverted bell-shaped capital) and flat, undecorated, square stone abacus together form a simple capital that supports a plain architrave. Above that, the frieze alternates between triglyphs and metopes as you scan horizontally. Triglyphs (meaning "three slits") are possibly a stylized throwback to the ends of cross beams originally used to support the roof. The metopes carried carved marble or terra-cotta panels depicting heroic narratives or images of the gods.

Occasionally, the Doric style has a slightly heavy look due to the thickness of columns such as those at the temples at Paestum, but such criticism cannot be leveled at the Parthenon, Athens, which appears perfectly balanced despite its monumental size.

An Enduring Legacy

The Doric order is seen mostly on the Greek mainland and in the Dorian Greek colonies in Italy. Modern use of this order can be seen in many public buildings, including the Old Patent Office in Washington, D.C.

STYLE FILE

Notable Features:
Fluted columns;
Absence of bases below the columns;
Undecorated capitals;
Plain architraves.

Major Influences:
Earlier Greek buildings and those of neighboring Persia and Egypt.

Where and When:
Greece and Italy; from 10th century BC.

BELOW: *The Doric temple of Athena (c. 500 BC), Paestum, Italy.*

THE IONIC ORDER

The Ionic order began about 550 BC. It has a lighter, more slender feel than the Doric, yet is often richly carved and decorated, and includes elaborate, tiered bases for its columns (which are missing entirely from Doric columns).

STYLE FILE

Notable Features:
Scrolled capitals;
Scalloped fluting at top
and base of columns;
Slimmer architraves;
Carved friezes.

Major Influences:
Ancient Greek buildings
in the Doric order.

Where and When:
Turkey and Greece; from
5th century BC.

Scrolls and Scallops

As with the other orders, the Ionic is quickly identified by its capital, which curves into scrolls (or volutes) at its edges to frame the top of the column. The column fluting is scalloped at the top and bottom, and the architrave is slimmer than in the Doric order. On the frieze, a band of stone, often richly carved with figures, replaces the Doric metopes and triglyphs.

Ionia and Beyond

The Ionic order originated, and is most commonly found, in the Greek cities of Ionia (the islands and coast of Asia Minor, now western Turkey). Invented around 550 BC, it was perfected in the early fifth century BC and adopted on the Greek mainland later in the same century. Some of its finest examples are in Athens, such as the Erechtheion, built in marble between 421 and 406 BC.

BELOW, RIGHT: Caryatids took the place of simple columns in some temples, including at the Erechtheion, which is part of the Acropolis in Athens.
BELOW: Fluted ionic columns, with volutes, at the Erechtheion.

THE CORINTHIAN ORDER

The Corinthian was the last of the orders to be developed; it flourished during the Hellenistic period (fourth to first centuries BC), and its lavish carving and decoration became a hallmark of the Roman architecture that followed.

The New Leaf

The order's main distinguishing feature is an echinus (*see* page 17) that is lavishly decorated with serrated acanthus leaves, palm leaves, and spirals. Small volutes at each corner give the capital the same appearance from all sides, making it better suited to corners than the Ionic capital.

Monumental Style

Early, and subtle, examples of the Corinthian capital can be seen on the Choragic Monument of Lysicrates in Athens, completed in 334 BC. Initially this style was used primarily for interior columns. The earliest example of a Corinthian capital used as the sole exterior column order is probably the temple of Olympian Zeus in Athens, completed in the second century BC. Among the grandest surviving structures of Corinthian order is the Temple of Bacchus at Baalbek, Lebanon—until the Classical revivals began.

ABOVE AND BELOW: *Corinthian columns. The elaborate capitals below are from the Temple of Artemis, Jerash, Jordan.*

STYLE FILE

Notable Features:
Lavishly decorated echinus (inverted, bell-shaped capital); Carved leaves and spirals as decorative motifs; Volutes at capital corners.

Major Influences:
Previous orders of ancient Greek architecture.

Where and When:
Greece, Roman Empire; from c. 350 BC.

GREEK TEMPLES

Classical Greek architecture achieved its most perfect form in the temple—deceptively simple, symmetrical, and clean buildings, partly open to the elements and carefully sited to blend harmoniously with sky and landscape.

STYLE FILE

Notable Features:
Rectangular plan
(occasionally, circular);
Raised structure;
Roofs supported by
columns;
Symmetrical design;
Mathematical formality;
Decorated pediments;
Front and rear porches;
Built of marble or other
type of stone;
Painted in bright colors.

Where and When:
Throughout the ancient
Greek Empire; fifth to
first centuries BC.

ABOVE: *The Theseion was a Doric temple dedicated to Hephaestos and Athena in the Agora—the very heart of ancient Athens, its administrative and social center. The Agora was excavated from 1859 through the early twentieth century, and the Theseion is one of the best-preserved structures there: indeed, it is among the most intact ancient Greek temples ever to have been excavated.*

The Temple Structure

The classic form of the temple is a rectangular stone or marble building, raised on a plinth (or stylobate). The columns rising from around the edge of this plinth are topped by capitals that actually support the entablature (unlike many Roman temples, whose roofs are supported by walls, with columns embedded into them solely for decoration). A low-pitched roof, usually of wood covered by terra-cotta tiles, was supported by the entablature, and the triangular ends of the roof under the eaves were filled by a pediment, which was decorated or carved. Typically, a front porch (*pronaos*) and a back porch (*opisthodomos*) sandwiched the enclosed part of the temple (*cella*), which formed an inner sanctum for worship.

ABOVE: *The Parthenon, Athens, perhaps the best-known temple of the entire architectural legacy of ancient Greece.*

BELOW: *The surviving columns and lintels at the Temple of Poseidon, Cape Sounion, Greece. The supportive function of the columns under the lintels is clearly evident in these temples; the Romans would alter the column's role gradually to emphasize the decoration.*

Function and Decoration

The enclosed temple space, or *sanctum*, was dominated by a statue of the god to whom the temple was dedicated. Antechambers for offerings to the gods or storing treasure were also sometimes included.

We now see these temples as austere white or gray ruins, devoid of life, against blue Grecian skies. But in ancient Greece they would have been bustling with life and highly decorated—painted in bright reds, blues, and golds to create effects that may even appear gaudy to the modern eye.

ROMAN STYLE

Roman architecture combined practicality and technical brilliance with Greek styles to create a new public architecture for a military empire. As the Romans conquered and subdued the known world from Syria to Spain, Britain to Libya, they projected power and maintained prosperity via a complex built environment.

ABOVE: *The magnificent Arch of Constantine, Rome: a lavishly decorated status symbol.*

STYLE FILE

Notable Features:
Decorative columns
 and pilasters;
Corinthian-order carvings;
Arches, both supporting
 and decorative;
Domes;
Barrel vaults;
Concrete and stone.

Major Influences:
The ancient Etruscans
 and Greeks.

Where and When:
Europe, the Middle East,
 and northern Africa;
 c. 100 BC to AD 500.

Scale and Sophistication

The most impressive Roman buildings do not so much complement nature as impose themselves on it. While the Greek theater nestles into the hillside, barely disturbing its contours and relying on a natural vista for a scenic backdrop, Roman theaters like the Colosseum often rise from a flat urban landscape, with huge walls and elaborate systems of tunnels, gates, and ramps to service the action in the auditorium.

While such scale and sophistication are symbolic of Roman architecture, more mundane structures were just as important. The roads, sewers, bridges, and basilicas (judicial and administrative buildings) that supported commerce, military expansion, and urban life were just as central to the Roman legacy as the huge amphitheaters and temples that we often associate with its architecture.

Corinthian Columns

Roman architects had a special fondness for the more decorative Corinthian order and the composite orders derived from it. The lavish, flowery abundance of the Corinthian capital was generally preferred to the elegant curves of the Ionic capital, and the simple austerity of the Doric was almost entirely shunned.

Engaged Columns and Pilasters

A classic Roman stylistic device was to turn the structural column into a decorative feature. Strong walls would bear the load, while columns were embedded into the walls to give a superficial resemblance to Greek models. Sometimes the columns were squared off to become pilasters. An interesting example is the Great Temple of Petra in modern Syria.

Engaged columns and pilasters were used liberally in the Classical revivals of later centuries to evoke a Classical aesthetic when a more practical solid wall was needed to enclose an interior space. There are many such examples dating from the Victorian era.

ELABORATE CAPITALS

This detail photograph illustrates a Corinthian capital with acanthus decoration at the triumphal Arch of Constantine, Rome.

BELOW: *This painting, featuring Caesar, illustrates the grandeur of ancient Rome's architecture.*

THE ROMAN ARCH

Nothing is more symbolic of Roman architecture than the arch. This simple load-bearing device was developed in Mesopotamia and was known to the Greeks, but rarely used by them. The Romans used it extensively.

ABOVE: *Ruins of a Roman arch in Palmyra, Syria.*
BELOW: *The aqueduct at Segovia, Spain, late first-century AD.*

Ancient Rome's Iconic Arch

The Romans built highly elaborate triumphal arches with no practical purpose other than to commemorate victories and express the gratitude of Rome to its heroes by providing a ceremonial portal through which to parade prisoners and treasure. The triumphal arch of Septimius Severus in Rome's Forum is perhaps the best example, with its massive engaged columns and wide central arch flanked by two smaller arches, all bearing a monumental architrave carved with a dedication. Such arches have inspired many modern imitations, including the arch in New York City's Washington Square, London's Marble Arch, and the Arc de Triomphe in Paris.

Aqueducts

The most impressive Roman arches, however, are those constructed for practical, rather than ceremonial, purposes. The aqueducts that slaked the Roman Empire's thirst for water were enormous water-carrying bridges constructed almost entirely of long series of arches, often stacked layer upon layer, striding across broad river valleys. They brought water many miles from mountain springs to urban centers, and some still stand 2,000 years later, including the Pont du Gard near Nîmes in southern France.

DOMES AND BARREL VAULTS

By using domes and barrel vaults the Romans were able to create large covered spaces that had an open feel, without the need for central supporting columns—impressive and significant developments that are still in use today.

ABOVE AND BELOW:
Interior domes and arches at the
Pantheon (above) and St. Peter's
Basilica (below), both in Rome.

The Dome

The dome is another iconic Roman expression, informing many of the most impressive public and ecclesiastical structures of the late Renaissance and early Modern period—from the Capitol in Washington, D.C., to St. Peter's in Rome and St. Paul's Cathedral in London.

The archetype of all these domes is the Pantheon in Rome. The Pantheon is a building of technical brilliance and precise mathematical proportions. Its single huge dome uses coffered concrete panels to reduce the weight, and the distance from floor to oculus (the circular hole in the top that lets in light) is the same as the diameter of the wall. Remarkably, it still stands today.

Vaulted Ceilings

Barrel vaults, sometimes known as tunnel vaults, are the most basic form of vault, or arched ceiling. They are essentially an extended series of arches forming long, curved ceilings, semicircular in cross section. Another way to envision these is to see the arch as the basic unit: a vault extends this shape to two dimensions and the dome, three.

Domes and barrel vaults were often used together in basilicas to create a large central space under a dome, with barrel-vaulted naves and aisles radiating out from this center. These new buildings often became the first churches, thereby laying the foundation for much subsequent church architecture in the Christian era. This arrangement can be seen in the interior view of St. Peter's, at right.

TEMPLES AND THEATRES

Roman temples often resembled their Greek predecessors in terms of their rectangular ground plan and surrounding colonnades, but Roman temples were usually raised on a high podium and accessed via a deep porch.

ABOVE: *The Temple of Bacchus at Baalbek, Lebanon, with its Corinthian-style colonnade.*
BELOW: *Ruins of the Roman Teatro Greco at Taormina, Sicily.*

Temples

Many early Roman temples look superficially similar to their Greek counterparts, but the Romans were less strict about following a single order and they eventually developed their own styles. A fine example is the Maison Carrée in Nîmes, dating from the first century AD. Like most Greek temples, the Maison Carrée follows a simple rectangular plan, with columns ringing the outside and a porch three columns deep. But it stands on a much higher podium, and there is no colonnade along the side. The supporting *cella* walls extend almost to the edge of the podium, engaging the Corinthian columns. As with many Roman buildings, the columns are purely for decoration.

STYLE FILE

Notable Features
Temples:
Rectangular ground plan;
Colonnaded, usually with
  Corinthian columns;
Raised on a high podium;
Accessed via a deep
  porch at one side only.

Theatres:
  Semicircular in plan, or
  oval or circular for
  amphitheatres;
Stacked layers of arches
  bearing the weight;
Self-supporting and not
  reliant on topography
  like Greek theatres
  (built in natural hollows).

Another such example is the Great Temple of Petra in modern Syria. Here, a temple facade is carved out of the sheer rock face, complete with engaged Corinthian columns of no structural use.

ABOVE AND BELOW: *Exterior and interior views of Rome's most recognized landmark, the Colosseum, originally known as the Flavian Amphitheatre.*

Theatres and Arenas

Unlike Greek theatres, which were built into naturally occurring curved hollows or dug into hillsides, Roman theaters were entirely self-supporting and could be built anywhere. The best-known and most spectacular example is the multilayered stone-and-concrete Colosseum (built AD 70–80) in Rome. This enormous, oval-shaped structure housed approximately 50,000 spectators. It is still a remarkably atmospheric structure today.

BYZANTINE AND ROMANESQUE ARCHITECTURE

The fall of Rome in AD 476 did not mean the end of the Roman Empire, which, since AD 303, had been ruled from Constantinople, far to the east. The Emperor Constantine had established his capital beside the Bosphorus, between Europe and Asia, in the old Greek trading colony of Byzantium. The empire administered from here has become known as the "Byzantine," but to its rulers it was just the Roman Empire as before. The continuities with Classical Rome are clear in the majestic forms of Byzantine architecture, as they would be in the "Romanesque" style that subsequently swept across western Europe.

OPPOSITE: *An interior view of the central dome of the Byzantine Kariye Museum, Istanbul, Turkey, which is renowned for its opulent mosaics.*

BYZANTINE

Unlike ancient Rome, Constantinople was conceived as a Christian capital. Its greatest monuments were to be its churches. That bias can be overestimated— over time, religious sites would be spared, while secular buildings were cleared—but the pre-eminence of ecclesiastical architecture is still clear.

STYLE FILE

Notable Features:
Rounded arches;
Domes;
Interior mosaics.

Major Influences:
Roman technologies;
Christian spirituality.

Where and When:
Constantinople
(Istanbul, Turkey) and
the Byzantine Empire in
eastern Mediterranean
and Near East;
c. AD 400–1453.

Body and Soul

Byzantine builders matched their Roman predecessors in ambition and accomplishment, taking techniques like the arch and dome to new levels of refinement. To the massive monumentalism of their forebears, however, they added a new and paradoxical dimension, creating impressions of quite eerie ethereality. Typically, the Byzantine structure appears squat and solid from the outside; within, though, the impression is of weightlessness and light. Another Roman technique—that of mosaic—was used to shimmering effect to give an extraordinary sense of spiritual transcendence.

ABOVE: *The Byzantine mosaics of the Cefalù Cathedral, Sicily, Italy, were created by craftsmen from Constantinople.*

RIGHT: *The Kariye Museum, Istanbul. Originally built as a Constantine church, it was later modified and used as a mosque.*

The Basic Basilica

The basic form for the Christian church was taken over from that of the Roman basilica—the rectangular room in which a magistrate or public figure gave audiences. Long and open, with colonnaded aisles at either side, it allowed large congregations to come together and mingle freely. Another popular ground plan was that of the Greek cross (in which each arm is equal). The obvious Christian symbolism apart, this layout offered the ideal basis for the building of impressive domes.

The Dome from Rome

The great problem with any dome is that of controlling the outward thrust of all that unsupported weight. The use of tapering triangular "pendentives" allowed this thrust to be directed downward. The word "pendentive" literally means "hanging," and such structures really do seem to be suspended in the air. Vast loads could be distributed around arched windows and held up by gigantic supports, while still conveying an impression of gravity-defying grace.

ABOVE: *The magnificent Hagia Sophia ("Holy Wisdom"), whose minarets were added upon its conversion from church to mosque.*

THE HAGIA SOPHIA

It "seems not to rest upon solid masonry, but to cover the space with its golden dome suspended from heaven," marveled Procopius of the new Church of Hagia Sophia. Built 532–37 in Constantinople by the emperor Justinian, this famous church (which was converted into a mosque under Ottoman rule) represents the Byzantine achievement at its height. So daring was its design, however, that it twice collapsed and had to be rebuilt. The dome we see today was completed in 1346.

ROMANESQUE

Romanesque architecture takes its name from its use of the rounded arches so popular with the Romans, but beyond that the similarity is superficial. European architects in the tenth and eleventh centuries created their own distinctive style of architecture, producing buildings of great dignity and simplicity.

STYLE FILE

Notable Features:
Simple construction;
Heavy walls, either with
small window openings
or windowless;
Rounded barrel vaulting
supported by columns
within;
Rounded arches (known
as Romanesque arches);
Decorative porticoes;
Churches mostly built on
basilica plans.

Major Influences:
Roman buildings,
especially their arches.

Where and When:
Western Europe
(Carolingian Germany,
France, northern
Italy, and Spain);
c. 1000–1100.

A Virtue of Necessity

The Europe of the first millennium had lost touch with what should have been its inheritance of Classical learning—including the great manuals of Classical architecture. Builders worked by trial and error, then, and many of the features of the Romanesque style reflect the practical steps they found to accommodate these theoretical limitations. The rounded arch, for example, had been prized by the Romans on aesthetic grounds: it was not an especially efficient way of bearing loads. Hence the squat forms of so many Romanesque structures, their massive, windowless walls and the ranks of thick-set columns to be seen within. But architects of the time understood clearly how to make these limitations a source of strength: Romanesque buildings seem impressive now in their unity and restraint.

Opposite, above: *The Basilica of San Lorenzo Fuori le Mura, Rome, before it was destroyed in World War II (it has since been rebuilt). The campanile (twelfth century) and portico (c. 1220) are typically Romanesque.*

Right: *A Romanesque abbey with notable Byzantine and Armenian influences, San Vittore della Chiuse (early eleventh century) in Genga, Italy.*

SANTIAGO DE COMPOSTELA

The tomb of the Apostle James made this cathedral in Galicia, Spain, one of medieval Christendom's most important places of pilgrimage. Its imposing tunnel-like interior makes up in atmosphere what it lacks in decorative ebullience; light streams sparingly in through windows set high above buttressing aisles. The blankness of the exterior walls is broken up by ornamental arches; the main portals are richly ornamented with sacred statuary.

RIGHT: *Lorsch Abbey, near Worms, Germany, was one of the most prominent abbeys of the Carolingian Empire. This polychromatic gatehouse is a notable landmark of early Romanesque architecture.*

Simplicity

Romanesque architects were at their ease with rectangular forms, so the basilica plan remained popular for churches; columned aisles and chapels could readily be added around the sides. The result was frequently cruciform, with perhaps a semicircular apse at the eastern end for the main altar. Ceilings were carried by simple, semicircular arches, or barrel vaulting. Towers tended toward stubbiness—construction techniques simply did not allow for anything more slender and tall.

NORMAN

The Norman style of Romanesque architecture was developed in Normandy, northern France, and in the lands the Normans dominated during the eleventh and twelfth centuries—especially England, following the conquest of 1066, but also Wales, Scotland, Ireland, Italy and Malta.

Solid and Strong

While the Normans built timber structures, it is the great stone keeps, monasteries and cathedrals that remain today, and these are characterized by their seemingly impregnable solidity, massive size, and simple geometry. Like all Romanesque architecture, this was essentially austere; nowhere more so than on their highly functional castles and keeps. In a cathedral or abbey, the blankness of an external wall may have been broken up by the addition of a portico, or nonload-bearing arches or pilasters may have been incorporated for decorative effect. But these buildings impress most by virtue of their strength and dignity.

When the master masons learned the use of groin vaults—intersecting barrel vaults set at right angles, enclosing a square space known as a "bay"—designs began to change.

Increased Elaboration

The groin vault opened up many new possibilities. The bay became the basic unit of ground-plan design. Groin vaults were built to be mutually buttressing, which allowed main walls to be less massive than previously. In turn, this gave Norman builders a new freedom to include more and larger windows, with more elaboration, inside and out. England's Durham Cathedral is an early example, while Sicily's Monreale (see feature) is considered the greatest Norman cathedral.

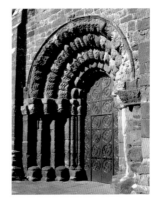

TOP: *The cloisters at Monreale Cathedral, Sicily, Italy.*

ABOVE: *Concentric bands of masonry decoration over large entrances are another hallmark of the Norman style, as seen here at St. Bees Priory, England.*

OPPOSITE: *Durham Cathedral, viewed from the south. It features perhaps the earliest use of ribbed groin vaults.*

LEFT: *The four-turreted Norman keep (1127) of Rochester Castle, defending southeastern England.*

LATE ROMANESQUE

In southern Europe—especially Italy—Roman ruins remained an ever-present influence, and for a long time architects kept closely to established forms. Farther north, however, builders were increasingly emboldened by their mastery of construction techniques and were setting their sights higher—literally.

STYLE FILE

Notable Features:
Groin vaulting;
Clerestory windows;
Increased use of
  (semi)circular floor plan;
Arcades and tracery.

Major Influences:
Roman, Romanesque
  and Norman buildings.

Where and When:
Throughout the
  Romanesque area,
  though architects in
  the north (France and
  Germany) were often
  the most innovative;
  c.1100–1300.

ABOVE: *St. Paul's Cathedral (13th century), Münster, Germany.*
BELOW: *The towers of Tournai Cathedral, in a World War II photograph.*

Increased Elaboration

The buttressing effect of groin-vaulted side aisles freed architects to build taller structures and design them with greater creativity. Germany's Speyer Cathedral, near Bamberg, is a particularly fine example. At the eleventh-century Abbey of Cluny, France, the square bays were replaced at the eastern-apse end by circular forms, but the chapels still radiated outward from the center, giving a beehive effect. Belgium's Tournai Cathedral (1146–1325) bridged the Romanesque period and the high Gothic. Both styles are clearly evident in the finished building: the clustering towers display Romanesque restraint, as does the rounded apse and the vaulted nave, while more exuberant additions were built later.

SANT'AMBROGIO, MILAN

Built about the same time as Pisa's *duomo*, Milan's Sant'Ambrogio is altogether a more chaste affair, giving the traditional Romanesque stylistic restraint a new lease of life. The use of "rib vaulting"— groined vaults with diagonal ribs criss-crossing at the center—gives a sense of dynamism and rhythm, without intro-ducing any feeling of fuss or clutter, and looks forward to the vaulting revolution that would follow during the Gothic age.

BELOW: *Two views of the* Piazza del Duomo *(or* Piazza dei Miracoli)*, Pisa: the baptistery (left, with cathedral behind); and the tower (right), with detail of the cathedral, foreground.*

Enduring Values

After the fall of the Roman Empire, Italy went its own way, Pisa in particular becoming associated with a highly ornamented—yet essentially conservative—interpretation of Romanesque styles. Its façade festooned with ornamentation—pilasters stacked above, blind arches below—Pisa's cathedral was cer-tainly not restrained, but strip away the exter-nal extravagances, and what remains is a boxy basilica, with square side chapels, its lower orders straightforwardly Romanesque. The oval dome at its center is striking, and sug-gests a strong Byzantine influence—an impression only heightened by the interior mosaics. Alternating patterns of dark and light marble lend a further sense of variety to the interior, without disrupting its simplicity.

The famous leaning *campanile,* or tower, was built at the end of the twelfth century. With blind arches at its base and tiers of columns around its upper stories, its design echoes that of the cathedral proper. The nearby baptistery and camposanto (cemetery) were also largely built in the twelfth century.

ISLAMIC ARCHITECTURE

"Whoever builds a mosque, desiring thereby God's pleasure, God builds the like for him in paradise." The words of the Prophet Muhammad (c. 570–632) were to find a concrete response from the seventh century onward, as Arab armies extended the frontiers of the Islamic world. By 750, the Umayyad Caliphate stretched from the Indus to southern Spain; a new architecture expressed the values of this new order. Its most characteristic feature was, not surprisingly, the mosque, but Muslim architects also built magnificent libraries, bath houses, palaces, and administrative centers, achieving a beautiful balance of spirituality and splendor.

OPPOSITE: *The modern Jumeira Mosque in Dubai, United Arab Emirates, is a beautiful building whose design draws on traditional Islamic styles.*

UMAYYAD AND ABBASID

When the Prophet Muhammad died, he was succeeded by a series of *khalifahs* ("representatives") or caliphs, whose authority was both worldly and religious. The caliphate reached its greatest size under the Umayyad Caliphate (661–750), whose capital was in Damascus, Syria. The Umayyad was followed by the Abbasid Dynasty, based in their glittering capital at Baghdad, in present-day Iraq.

STYLE FILE

Notable Features:
Mosques, with minarets and domes;
Interior prayer halls and courtyards;
Minbar pulpits and prayer niches (*mihrabs*);
Nonfigurative, decorative art, becoming increasingly extravagant.

Major Influences:
Basic form of mosque was derived from Muhammad's own house in Mecca. Other influences include Roman temples, Byzantine churches and decorative motifs from Central Asia.

Where and When:
Central Asia, the Mideast, north Africa, and southern Spain; c. 630–1258.

A Sacred Space

The word "mosque" comes from the Arabic *masjid*, "place of prostration." As such, the key feature of any mosque was the minaret, a soaring spire from which the muezzin sang out the call to prayer. Within were rooms for teaching, a *haram* (prayer hall) and often an arcaded *sahn*, or open courtyard. The entire structure was designed so that one wall of the *haram* faced the holy city of Mecca, the Prophet's hometown and the place of his first divine inspiration. An imposing *minbar*—like the Christian pulpit—represented the stepped platform from which Muhammad had first preached; beside it, arched prayer niches were let into the wall. Along other walls were fountains at which worshippers could perform their ritual ablutions.

The Qubbat al-Sakhra (Dome of the Rock) marks the spot of the Prophet's *miraj*, or mystic journey. The décor is distinctly Islamic, but the golden dome is inspired by the great Byzantine basilicas, such as Hagia Sophia (*see* page 31).

Abstraction and Ornamentation

The Great Mosque of Damascus (709–15), Syria, is one of the great achievements of the Umayyad dynasty; built on the site of a former Roman temple and Christian church, it has Byzantine-style mosaics. But since Muhammad had disapproved of figurative art, regarding it as usurping God's role as creator, the decoration (like all Islamic art) avoids representative images and icons. Instead, like many mosques, it is decorated with beautifully elaborate, rhythmically repeating geometric patterns and stylized calligraphic verses from the Qur'an.

Founded in 762, Baghdad was named the "City of Peace." At its center stood the Grand Mosque and Caliph's Palace; four main roads radiated outward. The relocation of Islam's capital was significant: Damascus had belonged to the Byzantine world, but Baghdad stood on the threshold of Persia and central Asia.

The Abbasid move to Baghdad brought Eastern influences to Islamic decoration. It was during this time that the stylized vegetal forms known as "arabesque" style developed. Abbasid craftsmen worked in silk, wood, and stone, but the most astounding effects were coaxed out of carved and painted plaster and stucco.

A SPIRAL MINARET

Between 836 and 862, Baghdad was replaced as the Abbasid capital by Samarra, whose Grand Mosque (848–52) represents an extra-ordinary homage to the builders of ancient Mesopotamia. Its unique spiral minaret clearly echoes the great ziggurat pyramids that were built by the people who established the world's first known civilizations between the Tigris and Euphrates Rivers.

TOP LEFT: *The Kadhimiya Mosque, in northern Baghdad.*
ABOVE: *The Minaret of the Bride stands by the northern gate of the Umayyad Mosque, or Great Mosque of Damascus.*
OPPOSITE: *The Dome of the Rock (begun in 685), with its gleaming golden dome and intricate exterior ornamentation, is a landmark of Jerusalem.*

ISLAM IN AFRICA

The African continent is divided by the Sahara, and the Muslim architecture of the two regions, although sharing a religion, is quite distinct. The fortifications and crowded streets of North Africa testify to a cosmopolitan and often volatile history, while the Subsaharan mosques have been uniquely adapted to the region.

At the Crossroads

The Islamic countries of North Africa have seen many invaders: Phoenicians, Greeks, Romans, Arabs, medieval Europeans and Ottomans. As a result, much of the architecture has a defensive nature. High, thick walls, with narrow or no windows are common features in both religious and civil buildings, such as the Cairo Citadel in Egypt and the Mosque of Uqba in Tunisia.

The kasbah, a walled citadel, is a common feature of many North African cities. These were often located on a hilltop or near a harbor for defensive reasons, where a local leader to seek shelter in times of unrest. Among the most famous are the kasbahs in Algiers, Algeria, and Marrakech, Morocco.

RIGHT: *Mosque of Uqba, Tunisia.*
OPPOSITE: *The great mosques at Djenné (above) and Timbuktu (below, the Djingareiber Mosque), both in Mali.*
BELOW: *Kasbah of the Udayas, a UNESCO world heritage site in Rabat, Morocco.*

Magnificent Mud Mosques

The mosques of Subsaharan Africa are among the most distinctive in the world, due to the use of mud-brick as the primary building material. These "mud mosques" have a unique and arresting appearance: they are thick-walled, relatively low buildings, with large, towerlike minarets. The walls and roofs are supported with wooden beams, which often protrude from the exterior surface; combined with the mud-plaster coating, this creates a somewhat forbidding, fortresslike effect. Some of the finest such mosques are in Mali, including the oldest, the Djingareiber Mosque ("the big mosque"), which was built in 1325 in Timbuktu, a Tuareg settlement that became a center of Islamic learning from the late fourteenth century. The imposing structure is thought to be the first example of this style, and the continent's oldest mosque.

Another significant landmark is the Great Mosque at Djenné, which is the world's largest mud-brick structure. Originally built in the thirteenth century, the current mosque dates from 1907. Mud mosques require frequent maintenance, to repair the damage of rains; the wooden beams serve as built-in scaffolding.

MOORISH ARCHITECTURE

Andalusia, southern Spain, was from the end of the eighth century the stable, prosperous—and Islamic—kingdom of al-Andalus. Under the Moors—Arab and Berber invaders who had made the short crossing from north Africa—some of the world's most beautiful monuments were built here.

STYLE FILE

Notable Features:
Horseshoe arches, often lobed and constructed with polychrome patterning;
Domes;
Mosaics;
Lasting legacy a distinct *mozarabic* influence on the Spanish architecture (even ecclesiastical) of later, Christian times.

Major Influences:
Umayyad;
Abbasid.

Where and When:
In the late 8th and 9th centuries, Moorish influence extended over much of Spain; thereafter increasingly confined to Andalusia until the 13th century.

The Damascus of the West

Al-Andalus was the one part of the Islamic empire in which the writ of the Abbasids never ran: it remained an Umayyad hold-out for several centuries. The Grand Mosque at Córdoba was accordingly modeled on that of Damascus, though the Moorish masterpiece had a character all of its own. It occupied the site of an old Visigothic church, much of whose masonry was incorporated into the northwest corner—so its "conversion" into a cathedral in 1236 is an irony.

It remains distinctly different, though: above columned aisles rise a riot of interlocking or stacked-up horseshoe arches, often delicately lobed for extra ornamental complexity; the alternating terra-cotta and cream slabs of their surrounds create a decorously festive mood. The *Mezquita* is massive—the third-largest mosque ever constructed—but the structure seems to float weightlessly, borne up by its slender columns and shapely arches. The sense of space

and airiness is exhilarating and is only enhanced by the abundant light that streams in from so many horseshoe-arched windows, set very high.

Within and Without

Light, air, and space are all key to the appeal of the Alhambra, a fortified palace complex on an outcrop above Granada. With its delicately ornamented stucco interior walls and ceilings, decorative screens, and ornate brickwork, this justly celebrated monument is an architectural showcase, but is perhaps most remarkable of all for its intimate courtyards and peaceful gardens. Space was as important to the Islamic architect as the solid walls and roofs that contained it; gardens were conceived as symbolic earthly paradises.

ABOVE AND BELOW: *The Alhambra of Granada, Spain.* OPPOSITE: *The Baños de la Encina castle was constructed by the Moors in 986.*

THE MUDÉJAR STYLE

The Moors who remained in Spain after the Reconquest were known as the Mudéjar. Dating from the 12th century, their buildings are sometimes called Brick Romanesque. Toledo, Aragon, and Teruel (below) have some of the best examples.

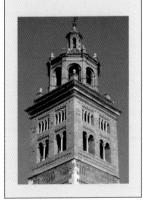

45

THE OTTOMAN STYLE

Steppe nomads, the Ottoman Turks emerged from the east to take Constantinople in 1458; as Istanbul it became capital of an Islamic empire. Ottoman architects took pride in their central Asian heritage and in the aesthetic principles of their Islamic creed, but also liked to see themselves as successors to the Byzantine emperors.

STYLE FILE

Notable Features:
Classic Islamic forms remained a given, but Byzantine influence formed taste for imposing domes and simpler decorative styles.

Major Influences:
Central Asian folk and Islamic religious traditions—but major impact of Byzantine models.

Where and When:
Centered on Istanbul, the Ottoman Empire covered much of the Mideast and southeastern Europe by the 16th century; in decline thereafter, it did not collapse until 1918.

Recycling Styles

By now already a thousand years old, the Hagia Sophia was taken as a template for Ottoman architecture; the great basilica was itself reconsecrated as a mosque, and minarets were added. That it looks so convincing in its Islamized form only underlines the extent of the influence it had on subsequent Ottoman religious architecture— its influence on the stupendous Suleimaniye Mosque (1550–57) and Sultan Ahmet Camii or "Blue Mosque" (1609–16), for example, is unmistakable. The dome took clear pride of place as aesthetic centerpiece: Islamic architects appreciated its awesome grandiosity and gravity-defying poise, as well as the sense of spiritual

RIGHT: *Istanbul's "Blue Mosque" takes its name from the interior tilework rather than any feature visible on its exterior. The splendid seventeenth-century landmark was built by Sedefkar Mefmet Aga.*

THE MUSLIM MICHELANGELO

Sultan Suleiman I, "The Magnificent," made Istanbul one of the most splendid cities in the world, but he could never have done so without his court architect, Koca Sinan (c.1490–1588). Born into a peasant family, he trained as a military engineer before being entrusted with the task of turning Istanbul into Islam's greatest city. And it shows—his great bridges and aqueducts are in their functional way as impressive as his prestigious palaces, mosques, hospitals, colleges, and schools.

space it produced within. The interiors beneath such vast canopies were almost by definition dimly lit, but the soft rays that filtered down through the rows of little windows set high above played thrillingly on shimmering mosaics. In former times a figurative technique, mosaic lent itself strikingly well to the abstract and calligraphic designs of Muslim artists, who also found fascinating cross-fertilizations among mosaic, ceramic-tile, and other decorative media.

ABOVE: *The recently rebuilt Stari Most Bridge in Mostar, Bosnia, was created by Ottoman architect Mimar Hajruddin in 1566.*

BELOW: *A courtyard detail at the Topkapi Palace, Istanbul, which was an organic complex of buildings and gardens. It was converted into a museum in 1924.*

Gone, But Not Forgotten

Less immediately evident, but still significant, was the Ottomans' own central Asian artistic tradition. As nomadic pastoralists, the Turks had no background at all in architecture as such, but their weaving and craft traditions influenced later decorative styles. And some buildings—the pavilions of Istanbul's fifteenth-century Topkapi Palace, for example—make clear reference to the tents of former times.

PERSIAN ARCHITECTURE

Under the Safavid shahs of Iran in the sixteenth to eighteenth centuries, Islamic architecture reached one of its acknowledged high points. At Esfahan a capital was created that proclaimed the power and glory of the dynasty: its most famous monuments seem less like buildings than gigantic jewelry.

Ceramic Spirit

The Safavids promoted themselves as patrons of the arts: carpet-weaving and calligraphy both flourished in this period. So, too, did painting and illustration, including some stunning miniatures—often figurative, for the Safavids were wayward with regard to some of the traditional Islamic strictures. They were perhaps most famous, though, for their consummate skill with ceramics: heart-stoppingly beautiful effects were achieved through the technique of *cuerda seca*.

RIGHT: *The courtyard and pool at the Masjid-i'Jami Mosque, Esfahan, Iran. The mosaics are of typical Safavid colors.*

SHEIKH LOTFALLAH MOSQUE

Esfahan's Sheikh Lotfallah Mosque was built in the early 17th century, during the reign of Shah Abbas I, which was the very zenith of Safavid power. The illustration shows a detail of the entrance portal, but the whole gigantic structure was covered from top to bottom in this sort of staggeringly beautiful glazed-tile decoration, proof of the exhilarating life and energy to be found in the finest ornamental art.

This was a way of decorating tiles and bricks by applying a "dry cord" of wax and manganese in the chosen pattern and then filling the spaces so formed with colored glaze. Exquisite precision could be achieved, and individually worked tiles could be placed together to form astonishingly intricate designs on a massive scale. Esfahan's Masjid-i'Ali Mosque is the perfect example: though founded as early as the twelfth century, it was completely rebuilt and redecorated under Shah Ismail in the sixteenth century.

Safavid craftsmen also made mosaics out of single-colored tiles, which were typically blue or turquoise, though yellow, green, purple, pink, and white were also used. These "seven colors" (or *haft rang*) gave their name to the distinctive mosaic style that resulted— and again, the utmost delicacy could be reconciled with a grandiose scale.

ABOVE AND BELOW: *Stunning ceramic work at the Sheikh Lotfallah Mosque in Esfahan, Iran, in an entrance (above) and the interior of the dome (below).*

MUGHAL ARCHITECTURE

The Mughals were named for their Mongol origins, though their founder, Babur, was descended from a line long established in Turkestan. So the cultural influences he carried with him when he invaded India in 1526 were above all Persian and Islamic, though being open-minded rulers, the Mughals embraced indigenous styles as well.

LEFT: *A Mughal mausoleum in Delhi, India.*
OPPOSITE, TOP: *Detail of a typical Mughal dome*
OPPOSITE, BELOW: *The sublime Taj Mahal, with its reflecting pool, in a nineteenth-century photograph.*

A Taste for Tombs

Art lovers, broad-minded thinkers, *bon viveurs* and skilled gardeners, the Mughals were definitely one of the more life-affirming historical dynasties. It is somewhat ironic, therefore, that their main architectural legacy should turn out to have been the vast mausoleums that they built at sites across northern India. One fine early example is the Adham Khan Tomb, part of the Quwwat-al-Islam complex, outside Delhi. Above octagonal walls with ogee arches rises a massive, broad-based dome; the result is imposing, if at the same time a little impersonal. Despite its being a bulky structure, when seen at close range, it turns out to be ornamented with surprising exuberance, albeit with both delicacy and discretion.

STYLE FILE

Notable Features:
Use of red sandstone and (especially later) marble;
Accent on the explicitly monumental, including mausoleums;
Simple forms, extravagantly, but discreetly, ornamented.

Major Influences:
Islamic forms with Persian inflection;
Many decorative motifs derived from Hindu Indian traditions.

Where and When:
Centered upon northern India, the Mughal Empire extended from Turkestan to Bangladesh and through all but the southern-most part of India; 1500s to 1700s.

Growing Simplicity

Oddly, on the face of it—but it is in keeping with the way the Mughal style developed—the tomb of Abdur Rahim Khan in Delhi was conceived later, but seems simpler. Dating from the mid-seventeenth century, it is essentially a sandstone cube topped with a marble dome. It stands on what amounts to a vast stone plinth, across which spread stunningly landscaped gardens with lovely pools; the whole scene is clearly intended to be viewed as a totality.

THE TAJ MAHAL

The Taj Mahal was built between 1631 and 1648 by the Mughal emperor Shah Jahan at Agra, as a tomb for his beloved wife Mumtaz Mahal. A study in symmetry, its bulbous domes set off by straight and slender minarets on either side, it is classically viewed along a long reflecting pool. From a distance it presents a picture of simplicity, even chastity, an impression that is confounded at closer quarters when its marble slabs reveal a riot of ornamental carving in an extraordinary mélange of Hindu, Persian, Turkish, and Arabic styles.

TRADITIONAL ASIAN STYLES

Asia has been home to some of history's greatest and most glittering civilizations, and birthplace of some of the world's most venerable religions. The Silk Road and other trade networks made some nations cultural crossroads, while others, such as Japan, remained aloof for centuries. But everywhere there is a sense of continuity, with the influence of ancient principles and designs still evident today, both in their places of origin and wherever those influences traveled. Exotic temples to Buddha and Brahma, restrained Japanese designs, and Beijing's legendary Forbidden City: all represent the rich and varied heritage of the continent. Indeed, the sheer size of the area and the long history of civilization make it impossible to cover the built landscape of Asia in this volume. The following section is only the briefest of overviews, addressing those architectural styles that have had the greatest impact on the Western imagination. Many Asian countries are now world leaders in international contemporary architecture, and examples of the exciting new work being done can be found in the last chapter of this book.

OPPOSITE: *The Great Wall of China extends from the Jiayuguan Pass of Gansu Province in the west to the Shanhaiguan Pass of Hebei Province in the east, winding more than 4,000 miles in length.*

CHINESE TRADITIONS

A sense of self-sufficiency, even introversion, has been a consistent theme of Chinese history over millennia. For centuries so far in advance of the rest of the world that it saw little to be gained by outside contact, after the sixteenth century China sought to shut out European colonialism.

STYLE FILE

Notable Features:
Post-and-beam wood
   construction;
Curved overhanging
   eaves;
Horizontal emphasis.

Major Influences:
Ancient indigenous
   traditions;
Introduction of Buddhism,
   from 1st century AD.

Where and When:
China; c. 8th century BC
   to modern period—only
   very gradual change.

ABOVE: *The classic Chinese summer pavilion, its water-bound situation inviting quiet contemplation.*
BELOW: *The Temple of Heaven (1420), Beijing.*

Spatial Relations

In architecture, this has meant an adherence to essentially unchanging principles rooted in religious beliefs of great antiquity. Much architectural thinking is founded in the traditional lore of geomancy, which read mystic significance into the forms of the landscape and the orientation of buildings within it. Feng shui laid down comparable rules governing the internal disposition of rooms and even of furniture and other objects in them.

In the Balance

The key construction material was wood, the main method a simple one using posts and beams; this system made it easier to build wide than high. Architectural aesthetics made a virtue of necessity: there was an emphasis on the horizontal line, and symmetry and balance were prized far more than sheer size. The pagoda may be the most famous Chinese building form, yet, in fact, it stood out not only literally, but stylistically—and it, too, can be seen as a stack of low-rise layers. It is no surprise to find that the pagoda was originally an import from India, a version of the Buddhist stupa (see pages 58–59). Overhanging eaves, beautifully curved, completed the effect of understated elegance and simplicity.

Small Dwellings; Great Wall

The only manmade object that can be seen from space? Astronauts have disputed it, but there's no doubting that the Great Wall of China (see page 52) is a massive structure. Winding more than 4,000 miles along the northern frontier of the empire, it was intended to exclude the warlike nomads of the Steppes. A barrier of hard-packed earth was raised by Emperor Shihuangdi around 214 BC; the present structure was built of limestone and granite, cemented with egg whites and rice starch, by the Ming Dynasty.

Beyond the wall, the architecture of the western Steppes and high plateau includes a variety of indigenous ethnic dwelling styles (see pages 60–61), and temples influenced by Buddhist tradition (see pages 58–59).

ABOVE: *The Fudong Temple in Shanxi is the oldest remaining wooden pagoda in China.*
BELOW: *Gateway at the Putuo Zongching Temple, Heibei, showing a Tibetan influence.*

THE FORBIDDEN CITY

Built in the early 15th century by the Emperor Yung Lo, Beijing's Forbidden City is a palace complex that covers an area of 250 acres and has more than 10,000 rooms. Rectangular in plan, it is built around a North–South axis along which are the emperor's throne rooms, roofed with gold. Construction was in hardwood, but the most important buildings were raised up on terraces of granite and marble, built of vast blocks brought from quarries 30 miles away. Secrecy—key to the imperial mystique—was preserved by a 30-foot perimeter wall, which was itself surrounded by a 150-foot-wide moat.

JAPANESE TRADITIONS

Like that of China, an early influence, the architecture of Japan was long defined by the country's cultural and political isolation. In the century and a half since it opened up its borders, though, its people's ancient ancestral traditions have played a vital role in the development of international Modernism.

RIGHT: This apparently modern interior is at the 17th-century Katsura Imperial Villa in Kyoto. BELOW: Its cave setting protects this 14th-century Kamakura structure from the elements.

Architectural Autonomy

In the early centuries of the first millenium AD, Japan was notably influenced by Chinese culture, adopting not only the Chinese script and architectural styles, but also the Buddhist religion then dominant in China. This influence is revealed in the curved roofs with overhanging eaves, and in the post-and-beam method of construction, as well as ceramic roof tiles in early buildings.

Beginning in the ninth century, as more temples were constructed in rural areas, the irregular landscape, coupled with earthquakes and heavy rains, led to changes in building design. One such shift was the replacement of ceramic roofs with wooden ones. Another period of innovation was the Kamakura shogunate (1185–1333). Tokyo's Shofuku-ji is a unique example of this style: despite the two-story exterior appearance, the interior is a single open space. The roof is supported by cantilevers, steel support chisels, and flexible cypress. The result is an earthquake-resistant building that nonetheless has a light, airy appearance.

THE GOLDEN PAVILION

First built as a retirement home for Japan's ruling shogun in the late 14th century, Kyoto's Kinkaku-ji Temple subsequently became a Buddhist shrine. It makes a ravishing sight when the rising or setting sun glints on the gold leaf with which its eaves are coated, the shimmering waters of the lake only enhancing the effect. Atop a first story in what was already the anachronistic Heian style of the 11th century sits a second in the contemporary 14th-century manner. The third story, much the smallest, shows the direct influence of the Chinese architecture of the time.

ABOVE: *Kinkaku-ji Temple.*

A Sense of Space

In the architecture of Japan, as in China, balance is all-important, though in larger complexes a more sophisticated sense of symmetry may be displayed. In a typical temple group, for example, a tall tower may balance a low pavilion, the buildings complementing, rather than mirroring, one another. Architects worked with what is now known as "dynamic symmetry," proportions that seem natural—and are seen in all sorts of natural organisms, from spiraling seashells to the human body.

This appreciation of spatial relations for their own sake went along with the minimalist interior design so admired in the West in modern times. There was a strong sense, too, of the interplay between interior and outside space, which were often brought together by the use of balconies.

TEA HOUSES

Japan's tea houses first appeared in the 15th century, and are known as *chashitsu*. The design of the *chashitsu* is heavily influenced by Zen philosophy; it often resembles a rural cottage. The *chashitsu* is constructed of natural materials and usually has sliding wooden doors, with translucent paper-covered windows, and woven mats. Both *chashitsu* and the tea ceremony itself focus on simplicity and tranquility.

TEMPLE ARCHITECTURE

India is the birthplace of two of the world's oldest religions, Hinduism and Buddhism. Although Buddhism was mostly eradicated in India in the first millennium, it and Hinduism have spread throughout Asia. In both cases, traditional wooden building techniques were later translated in stone.

STYLE FILE

Notable Features:
Use of post-and-lintel stone construction; "Mountain" pyramids at center of Hindu temples; Mound-shaped stupas at center of Buddhist shrines and temples; Hindu temples highly ornate, with many statues and images.

Major Influences:
Hindu traditions stretching back 3,000 years; indigenous elements where Buddhism spread.

Where and When:
India from c.1000 BC; China; Southeast Asia.

ABOVE: *The 2,000-year-old temple of Mahabalipuram in Tamil Nadu, southern India.*
BELOW: *Hindu temples are usually richly decorated.*

The Mandir Mountain

Hinduism emerged over 3,000 years ago and has done much to fashion the character of modern India. Over the centuries it has been exported through much of Southeast Asia.

The Hindu *mandir* is a stone temple, typically raised on a stone terrace or plinth; this physical ascent mirrors the worshipper's spiritual ascent. The heart of any *mandir* is the *garbhagriha* ("womb chamber"), which contains the image of the god. Rising above this chamber is the pyramidal *shikhara*, representing Meru, the center of the Hindu cosmos.

Hinduism has many gods (and their avatars), and temples are often covered with exuberant carvings. Often brightly painted, these carvings give the temples a festive air, especially as it is not uncommon to find figures engaged in activities that Westerners would hardly consider appropriate!

ABOVE: *Rounded stupas at Borobudur, a 9th-century Buddhist site in Java, Indonesia.*
BELOW: *This is among the 300 Buddhist temples in the Thai city of Chiang Mai. Thai temples have tapered, pointed stupas and roofs.*

WAT MAHATHAT

Built in the 13th century in brick and stucco, Wat Mahathat was one of the most important shrines of the Sukhothai civilization; it stands in the northern part of modern Thailand. As at Angkor, the gigantic central stupa takes the form of a lotus—a plant revered because, while its roots lay in the mud, its exquisite flower strove upward to the light. It is surrounded by smaller stupas, eight at each of the four cardinal directions. There are several *viharas*, too, and many splendid statues: one seated Buddha is over 30 feet tall.

Last Resting Place of the Buddha

Siddhartha Gauthama, the Buddha, was born in 566 BC in modern-day Nepal. Renouncing worldly concerns, through self-denial and meditation he finally found "the way" to leave bodily preoccupations behind and attain the state of spiritual transcendence that he called nirvana, or "awakening." He made "the Great Passing Away" to the final nirvana aged 80, at Kusinara, India; at his request, his followers heaped earth over his cremated remains in the traditional manner. The resulting mound was the prototype for the stupa, the central feature of Buddhist shrines. Usually rounded (but pointed in Thailand), stupas are often crowned with a carved pinnacle that represents the bodhi tree under which the Buddha achieved enlightenment. The stupa also suggests Sumeru, the Hindu cosmic mountain.

The stupa is traditionally encircled by a stone-slab fence, the *verdika*, with ceremonial gates, or *toranas*, at the cardinal points. Large shrines will also have *viharas*—living accommodation for monks—and statues of the Buddha, seated in meditation or in the moment of death and the last nirvana.

ASIAN REGIONAL STYLES

Years of conquest, colonialism, and the ineluctable advance of globalization have contributed to the replacement of much of Asia's native architecture. Nonetheless, the native domestic building traditions reflect the diverse lifestyles and landscapes of the world's largest continent.

RIGHT: *Housing in mountainous western China (above) and a Mongolian yurt (below).*

THE VERSATILE YURT

The domestic *ger* (the Mongolian name for a yurt) is reprised in the sacred architecture of Mongolia. Many of the earliest Buddhist temples were mobile *gers*; and when these later became permanent structures, many preserved the design of the nomad's home.

From Steppes...

The nomads of the Central Asian steppes had little use for a home that couldn't travel as easily as they did. So they developed the yurt, a portable home that could be easily put up or dismantled in a matter of hours. The circular building is made of a wooden lattice frame (the wood must be light for portability: trees don't grow on the steppes) with a felt covering. Ropes and the weight of the felt hold the structure fast. The sloping roof has a small opening at the top, originally to allow smoke out. The felt is traditionally made from the wool of the family's sheep, and the door faces south. Even today, some 30-40 percent of Mongolians make their homes in a yurt.

...To Stilts

Far from the arid steppes, in large parts of Southeast Asia people were most concerned with frequent flooding. Building houses on stilts was the best way to cope with the regular inundations. Specific details of design vary according to the cultural traditions and water levels, but there are shared features. These homes are built on stilts, wooden or bamboo poles that raise them high off the ground. They have steeply sloping roofs. The entire structure is made of bamboo or wood, with much of the structure prefabricated and assembled on site. The space underneath is used for storage or livestock.

Mountainous Regions

Across the Himalayas, from Pakistan to China, much of the the architecture reflects the Hindu, Islamic, and Buddhist influences described in other pages of this book. Simple shacks often serve as seasonal homes in high altitudes, with more permanent dwellings in the lower towns and villages, or else under the protection of fortified sites (see sidebar).

ABOVE: *Stilt houses on an island in Indonesia. Stilt houses are widely built inland, in Thailand and Vietnam, for example.*

DZONGS

Mostly found in the small Himalayan kingdom of Bhutan (as at Trongsa, below), *dzongs* are defensive fortresses on high, commanding sites, comprising massive, inward-sloping masonry walls surrounding a complex of courtyards, a temple, administrative and residential spaces. Pagoda-style roofs adorn the temple and towers. Walls are mostly white; windows and a decorative red stripe are positioned at wall tops.

GOTHIC AND MEDIEVAL ARCHITECTURE

The word "Gothic" was first used as an unflattering description by Italian architects of the Renaissance, anxious to distance themselves from what they saw as the irredeemable barbarism of the Middle Ages. The Goths, to them, had been one of the warlike Germanic tribes that had brought about the destruction of Rome and of the Classical achievement. The label was unjust—to the Goths themselves (a fascinating people), but still more to the creators of Europe's great castles and cathedrals. The medieval period is now widely recognized as a golden age of European architecture; the Gothic style would enjoy a major revival in the nineteenth century.

OPPOSITE: *The thirteenth-century Montale Fortress in the tiny Republic of San Marino is an excellent example of medieval defensive architecture. The independent enclave is located in northern Italy.*

MEDIEVAL FOUNDATIONS

The early medieval period was a time of endemic instability and violence in Europe. Local lords jostled and fought for regional power and kingship. The only real order was to be found in the organization of the Roman Catholic Church.

Feudal Strongholds

The kings and barons of early medieval times were only a step or so up from what we would now call warlords: they had built their power bases by bullying and extortion. As formalized under the feudal system, the lord held his "manor," or local territory, in trust from his king, and had rights over its produce and its people's labor. In return, as the king's "vassal," he had a duty to support him in times of war and to raise and maintain fighting troops on his behalf. His life was strongly milita-rized, then, and his home was his headquarters: an important lord would have a small army of retainers. There was nothing showy about the medieval castle—the ornamental *châteaux* would come much later—these were utterly functional constructions, designed for defense.

ABOVE: *Batalha Monastery, Portugal (begun in 1386).*
BELOW: *Fort La Latte.*
OPPOSITE: *The "White Tower," part of the Tower of London.*

Towns and cities enjoyed a certain amount of autonomy, but this, too, might have to be defended. Local nobles resented their independence and coveted their wealth, so the fortifications around medieval cities were sorely needed.

Churches and Cathedrals

Only much later would the castle become predominantly a status symbol, but its church announced the wealth and prestige of the community from the start. Whether the abbey churches of the monastic orders or the cathedrals of increasingly wealthy and self-confident merchant cities, medieval churches were an expression of institutional and civic pride. It was in ecclesiastical architecture, then, that the most dazzling displays of virtuosity would be seen, and the most daring of artistic experimentation.

FORT LA LATTE

Fort La Latte was built in the 13th and 14th centuries, on a rocky outcrop almost 300 feet above the sea at Cap Fréhel, Brittany, France. Though updated at the end of the 17th century, it clearly conforms to medieval type, with its cylindrical keep and surrounding curtain wall. Impregnable from the sea, it is cut off by deep defiles on the landward side: when its drawbridge was up, it was virtually impossible to storm.

MEDIEVAL FORTIFICATIONS

Self-defense

Medieval castles were essentially stone stock-ades—though the earliest examples would have been built of earth and wood. A "'curtain wall' enclosed a "bailey" or open area, in which—often on a motte, or mound—stood a massive "keep," the central tower. The main living quarters were here, along with essential stores and, if it could possibly be contrived, a well. The idea was that even if the curtain wall were to be breached, the keep could still be defended—if necessary, through an extended siege.

A Position of Strength

Natural features were exploited: wherever possible, castles were built on rocky outcrops, on islands, or beside ravines or rivers. Where no such features could be found, an artificial moat might be dug; this was crossed by a drawbridge that could be raised or lowered for access.

A Formidable Barrier

Stone walls were often many feet thick; sheer strength was important, but designs grew steadily in sophistication. Crenelations along the tops provided a degree of protection to defenders on high battlements; narrow slits were cut in curtain walls and towers from which arrows could be shot in comparative safety. Machicolations, projecting parapets with holes underneath, allowed boiling pitch to be poured over attackers attempting to scale walls. Towers stood out from walls to allow archers to cover the curtain wall; they were generally rounded for extra strength and to deflect missiles.

Town Walls

Towns and cities had fortifications of their own: they had seldom been sited with defense in mind, so each was surrounded by what amounted to a curtain wall. This, too, might have projecting towers placed at intervals. Big gates with guardhouses controlled the main roads in and out.

THE WALLS OF AVILA

Begun in 1090 by King Alfonso I, using the labor of Moorish prisoners, the walls of this central Spanish city run for well over a mile and have no fewer than ninety massive towers. In areas at peace, cities built their own walls, partly for prestige, though mainly for defense.

ABOVE: *Detail of machicolations at Spain's Coca Castle.*

LEFT: *Carcassonne, in southwestern France, is the textbook example of a medieval fortified city. Its castle and city walls, with towers and crenelations, protected the citadel from invaders from the eleventh century onward.*

OPPOSITE: *The thirteenth-century Dunluce Castle, County Antrim, Ireland, is located on a naturally defensive site on a rocky outcrop.*

GROWING INTO GOTHIC

As the twelfth century began, the Romanesque style still held sway in Europe, though its starkest simplicities had very gradually been left behind. It was inevitable, though, that an age in which both cities and monastic communities were growing in wealth and confidence would bring a new intrepidness in church design.

A Missing Link

The gulf between even a relatively elaborate Romanesque cathedral and a Gothic tour-de-force like that of Chartres, France, or Salisbury, England, may seem unbridgeable, but some churches do seem to represent an intermediate stage. One of especial interest is that of St. Denis, near Paris, a Romanesque construction given a Gothic makeover in 1137–44. The Romanesque influence remains clear inside, though groin vaults—once a "special effect"—are used more generally; and the windows have pointed arches instead of the rounded ones of old.

RIGHT: *Salisbury Cathedral, England: its richly detailed Gothic facade contrasts with the surviving Romanesque features.*

High Gothic

This was more than an aesthetic change: pointed arches redistributed weight, replacing much of the outward thrust with downward, allowing constructions to be taller and walls and columns to be more slender. The accent was now on verticality, an effect emphasized by the liberal use of pointed pinnacles and spires—even the grandest Romanesque monuments now looked squat and stubby.

Ornamentation

Freed to some extent from their load-bearing duties, walls could afford to be less solid: they could accommodate vast decorative windows of stained glass. No longer a space of gloom, the interior of the church became a canvas on which artists and craftsmen could express themselves exquisitely. There were stunningly sculpted saints' statues and fonts, and elaborately carved wooden pulpits, pews, and choir screens. Paintings depicted Judgment Day scenes and the fires of hell (devils also festooned the exterior in the form of ornamental water spouts or gargoyles). Stonemasons vied with one another to create the most extravagantly ornamented pinnacles and spires.

ABOVE: *The cathedral at Chartres, France, which combined the first use of flying buttresses, when building began in 1185, with later, extravagant features. The landmark is especially well-known for its carvings and stained glass.*

BELOW: *The cathedral in Segovia, Spain, built in the sixteenth century.*

SALISBURY CATHEDRAL

Southern England's imposing Salisbury Cathedral was built in the mid-13th century, but Romanesque elements still persist in its design. Its nave and side chapels, accordingly, are not particularly tall, and seem almost stolid by Gothic standards, though this just sets off the breathtaking verticality of the soaring spire.

FRENCH GOTHIC

As the Gothic style took root, it began to grow divergently, local variations becoming identifiable. Its birthplace, France, developed its own very special style.

BELOW: *Rayonnant Gothic at the magnificent cathedrals of St. Chappelle, Paris (left) and Reims (right, rose window).*

Rayonnant Gothic

One of the most famous cathedrals in the world, Notre Dame was built in Paris between 1163 and 1250—by no means an unusually lengthy construction by the standards of the day. Generations of workers would be involved in the building of a great medieval cathedral, which had implications for the way that it finally appeared. Clear and coherent overall conception is typically balanced by a surprising degree of license in decorative detail: scope for wood- and stonecarvers to express themselves. Notre Dame's west facade, in particular, presents the viewer with simple symmetries—but, on closer inspection, the exuberance of its decoration becomes clear. The arched doorways at ground level are thronged with saints and angels packed from top to toe; further figures form a line above, beyond which may be seen a stunning show of stained glass, centering on a magnificent rose window. These controlled explosions of color were an innovation in thirteenth-century France and were to prove so popular that the period is known as the Rayonnant ("radiating") period.

LEFT AND BELOW: *Notre Dame de Paris, one of the most recognized sacred buildings in the world. The western facade, famed for its elaborate carvings, is shown at left, and an ornamental grotesque, below.*

So magnificent is this facade that the soaring spire behind may only just be seen: you have to walk partway round the cathedral—and retreat to a distance—to see it clearly. Such a view reveals a nave and apse positively bristling with flying buttresses. The visual effect is spectacular; this late-twelfth-century innovation was another factor in Gothic architects' remarkable success in combining altitude with elegance.

The Flamboyant French

Just as French architects and patrons had taken the lead in introducing Gothic, they pushed it farther than those of most other European countries. Flamboyant Gothic, as exemplified by the great fifteenth-century cathedral at Rouen, in Normandy, follows established Gothic principles, but takes its decorative exhibitionism to breathtaking extremes.

STAINED-GLASS SCRIPTURES

Chartres Cathedral (mainly 13th century) is a magnificent Gothic cathedral by any standards; what makes it unique is its astonishing collection of stained glass. More than 100 windows cast a kaleidoscope of colored light into the interior, showing a huge range of figures and scenes from the Bible. Between its windows and abundant statuary, the cathedral was a visual text in which the illiterate could "read" both the goodness of the Savior and the glory of God.

71

ENGLISH GOTHIC

English architects followed the French style enthusiastically, but selectively: they loved the effects of height and weightlessness, but acquired the taste for florid ornamentation only slowly. They did, in the end, acquire it, though, even if the final, elaborate efflorescence of the Gothic in England was delayed by the dynastic struggle, the Wars of the Roses (1455–85).

STYLE FILE

Notable Features:
Flying buttresses;
Slender columns;
High, stained-glass
  windows;
Hammerbeam roofs;
Fan vaulting, growing
  ever more complex.

Major Influences:
Natural evolution out
  of early English Gothic;
Some influence from
  French Rayonnant
  and Flamboyant
  architecture.

Where and When:
England; late 13th to
  early 16th centuries.

ABOVE: *King's College Chapel, Cambridge.*
BELOW: *Detail above doorway, Westminster Abbey, London.*

Decorated Gothic

Corresponding with the Flamboyant period in France was what in England was known as Decorated Gothic, best exemplified today by Exeter Cathedral. First built in the early twelfth century, it was extensively rebuilt in the late thirteenth and fourteenth centuries, taking full advantage of architectural developments that by then had taken place. Hence, the systematic use of flying buttresses allows slender columns and a windowed wall to rise up sheer and support a sublimely intricate fan-vaulted ceiling.

Perpendicular Gothic

Fan-vaulting figures, too, in the famous chapel of King's College, Cambridge, widely seen as the masterpiece of the Perpendicular style. Begun in 1446, but not completed until the early sixteenth century, it has a simple rectilinear plan. All its complexity is reserved for its amazing decoration. Aside from some of the world's loveliest stained-glass windows, its finest feature is the exquisite counterpoint between its soaring verticals and the delicate profusion of its vaulting.

So complex is this fan vaulting, indeed, that we lose the sense that it is structural: rather than dividing up the ceiling, it dissolves it into a single sweep. In fact, the vaulting was having to do less work, since "hammerbeams" were spreading the load of the roof far more efficiently. Short horizontal and vertical beams, arranged like steps, braced one another, providing much more support. Hammerbeam construction could only be handled by the most skillful joiners, but it gave architects new freedom to explore the expressive possibilities of the vaulted ceiling.

GOTHIC GOES WILD

Henry VII's chapel in Westminster Abbey, London, was not built until the early 16th century; it is hard to resist the feeling that this is English Gothic's final fling. Erupting out of slender supporting columns, the whole ceiling seems a seething expanse of living energy, its lacelike tracery bewildering the eye, its pendants almost defying gravity.

BELOW: *The Decorated Gothic cathedral at Wells, Somerset.*

ITALY AND GERMANY

In early medieval Italy, Norman warlords were establishing a kingdom in what until then had largely been Byzantine territory. Germany, meanwhile, was riding high under its Ottonian emperors, and was disinclined to genuflect to French fashions. In both countries, then, essentially Romanesque traditions were allowed to continue.

Technically Gothic

Keen though they may have been to keep their architectural autonomy, architects in both countries learned from the Gothic innovators. They could not fail to be impressed by the way developments in vaulting allowed roofs to be raised higher—for greater space and airiness—and supported by slim columns and windowed walls.

Hence, for example, Florence's Santa Croce Church, built 1254–1442 to a T-shaped ground plan. Its lofty naves and chapels are supported by thin columns with pointed arches, though overall an un–Gothic simplicity and sobriety prevail. While Brunelleschi's dome has generally been seen as a starting point for Renaissance architecture, the city's cathedral was medieval in foundation. It, too, brings Gothic techniques to bear in service of a Romanesque ideal of understatement: the austerity is there; what has gone is the sense of stolid mass.

RIGHT: *The Old Town Hall (1386) in Bamberg, Germany, was built between two bridges. The old section features a typical steeply pitched roofline and half-timber construction, a technique that endured in Germany for several centuries. The central section of the building was rebuilt in the eighteenth century.*

HOUSE OF GOLD

One of Italy's finest examples of Gothic architecture is not a church, unusually, but a residence: the Ca'd'Oro ("Golden House") in Venice. Its beautiful arched loggias were originally gilded (hence the name), but even without that finishing touch it is still an impressive structure by any standards.

ABOVE: *The famous "Golden House," Venice.*

BELOW: *Cologne's high Gothic cathedral is the city's most famous landmark: interior and exterior views.*

Cologne Cathedral (mostly dating from the thirteenth century) is a useful reminder that German architects did not avoid the Gothic altogether, but it is very much the exception, rather than the rule. More typical was the *Hallenkirche* or "hall church," whose side aisles were raised so as to be almost the same height as the main nave, creating a vast and cavernously echoing space inside. Nuremberg's Frauenkirche is justly famous; with only a half-hearted hint of a spire, it is broad and barnlike in its basic shape, but bedecked with (plainly Gothic–inspired) points and pinnacles.

CENTRAL AND NORTHERN EUROPE

Lacking that special halo of religious and civic sanctity that surrounded the great cathedrals, much secular medieval architecture was swept away by later builders. Relatively poor in Gothic churches, Scotland fares better for surviving secular architecture—and there are fine examples, too, in some of the other historic cities of central and northern Europe, including Prague, in the Czech Republic.

STYLE FILE

Notable Features:
Groined vaulting and
  pointed windows;
Jetties (overhanging
  upper stories).

Major Influences:
Gothic techniques,
  often given "Germanic"
  interpretation;
"Hall church" model
  widely followed
  in the Baltic region.

Where and When:
Central and northern
Europe; 12th–15th
centuries.

Pride of Prague

The rich medieval inheritance of Prague includes a spectacular fourteenth-century Gothic cathedral, St Vitus's, as well as smaller ecclesiastical buildings and townhouses. Charles Bridge, much more than a river crossing, is another splendid example of Gothic design: each end is defended by a pinnacled tower.

Gothic Outpost

The Old Town of Tallinn, Estonia's capital, is an extraordinary monument to medieval times: most of its buildings date back to the thirteenth century. The wilder extravagances of Rouen Cathedral or Notre Dame are utterly alien to these sober merchants' houses, churches, and

guildhalls, but we find the same sense of everything straining upward toward the sky. Pointed arches abound; roofs are steeply raked and profiles, narrow. Yet if the Gothic influence extended here, it was refracted through the prism of German usage, before being brought north by the Teutonic Knights when they invaded the Baltic kingdoms in the thirteenth century.

ABOVE: *John Knox House, Edinburgh, Scotland.*
OPPOSITE: *Prague's landmark Charles Bridge.*
LEFT: *Tyn Church, Prague.*
BELOW: *Detail of a Gothic arch in Tallinn, Estonia.*

RENAISSANCE AND BAROQUE ARCHITECTURE

Did the Renaissance even take place? Recent scholarship has been skeptical, uncovering deep medieval roots for the apparent "rebirth" of the arts and sciences in fifteenth-century Italy. Writers and thinkers like Dante and Petrarch, as well as such great artists as Giotto, had been enhancing European culture for generations. Italian architects, for their part, surrounded by the ruins of the ancient past, had largely shunned the Gothic experiment in favor of a Romanesque style that kept Classical aesthetic tastes alive. Yet there can be no real doubt that the fifteenth century did see an explosive surge in artistic and intellectual activity in Italy, especially in a Florence flush with the profits of the wool trade. That city's growing political autonomy brought with it a more generalized increase in intellectual and creative confidence, and a new humanism that proclaimed the possibilities of the individual spirit.

OPPOSITE: *The Rialto Bridge (1588–91) over Venice's Grand Canal. Michelangelo and Palladio were among those who competed to design this expensive project, but the commission was awarded to Antonio da Ponte ("Antonio of the Bridge").*

THE RENAISSANCE

The Italian Renaissance of the fifteenth century was underwritten by economic prosperity: trade flourished, increasing wealth while extending cultural horizons; the principles of modern banking were imported from the Islamic world. Artistic patronage became a way of expressing the pride and prestige of a community or private magnate—and architecture was the most visible of the arts.

ABOVE: *Brunelleschi's* Duomo, *jewel of Florence, Italy.*

STYLE FILE

Notable Features:
Classical styles, including
 domes and arches;
Herringbone brickwork
 for greater strength.

Major Influences:
Roman ruins, still to be
 seen across Italy;
Rediscovered writings of
 Vitruvius and others.

Where and When:
Italy, spreading to France
 and beyond; 15th–16th
 centuries.

The Human Scale

"Study good architecture," Leonardo da Vinci urged the reader hoping to attain expertise in art; the proportions of a fine building, he said, had all the balance of the perfect human body. The human form was now accepted as the ultimate standard of beauty, just as the human mind was regarded as the ultimate guarantee of truth. Humanism flourished first in Italy, where wealthy families like the Medicis and the Borgias were lavishing patronage on artists, architects, and scholars. Their aim may have been self-glorification, but they ended up glorifying humankind. Soon these new values were spreading, first to France, and then to Germany, the Netherlands, the British Isles, and beyond.

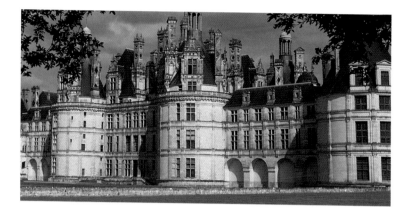

ABOVE: *Château de Chambord (1519–47), Loire Valley, France. Leonardo da Vinci is thought to have been involved in its design.*
BELOW: *Santa Maria Novella, Florence, was designed by Leon Battista Alberti (1404–72).*

IL DUOMO

Renaissance artists and scientists found in the Classical example a liberation from a medieval mindset schooled in subservient adherence to the authority of the Church. On the face of it, Italian architects had never abandoned their Classical inheritance, but in truth the Romanesque was really "Roman" only superficially. Not until Filippo Brunelleschi's great *Duomo*, or cathedral, in Florence (1420–36) do we see a triumphant recapturing of the Romans' structural engineering skills, and the enterprising spirit of the Classical builders.

Florence vs. Venice

A Florence dominated by the Medici family may have led the way to the Renaissance in Italy, but the port city of Venice was not to lag too far behind. A wealthy republic in its own right, Venice had a trading network extending far to the east, from where artistic influences were imported, along with material commodities. The headline story of the art and architecture of the Renaissance may be the rediscovery of the Classical heritage, but the impact of trade with the East (and, later, the Americas) was arguably as crucial.

HIGH RENAISSANCE

By the mid-fifteenth century, the ideas and achievements of the Early Renaissance masters were spreading out from Florence and Venice to other Italian states and cities. Fine palazzi and churches were built for wealthy patrons who desired not only lasting monuments, but perfectly planned cities.

STYLE FILE

Notable Features:
Similar to early
  Renaissance but with
  more ornamentation;
Domes and cupolas;
Carvings and statuary;
Geometric plans.

Major Influences:
Early Renaissance
  architecture;

Where and When:
Italy, c.1475 to 1550.

BELOW: *St. Peter's Basilica, Rome, perhaps the finest building of the Renaissance.*

Papal Power

Among the wealthiest and most ambitious of all Italy's patrons was the Catholic Church itself, and in the sixteenth century Rome's architectural treasures would become at least a match for those of Florence and Venice. Born in Urbino and gaining his reputation in Milan, Donato Bramante (1444–1514) moved in 1499 to Rome, where he made an indelible mark on the city. His *Tempietto* of San Pietro in Montorio, his cloister of Santa Maria della Pace, and his original design for St. Peter's Basilica would come to define Italy's High Renaissance. These masterpieces were built on complex geometric plans whose perfectly formal arrangements gave the deceptive impression of simplicity.

RIGHT: *Bramante's Santa Maria delle Grazie, Milan: not just a High Renaissance treasure, but home to Leonardo da Vinci's mural of the Last Supper.*

BELOW: *Sangallo the Younger's Church of Santa Maria di Loreto, Rome, is considered his greatest achievement.*

ROME'S DOMES

The Basilica of St. Peter's, built 1506–1626, is a contender for finest building of the entire Renaissance era—and not surprisingly, considering its glittering architects. Bramante won the competition for its design; he created the Greek cross plan and began work on the magnificent dome, which was inspired by the Roman Pantheon, but supported on four large piers rather than the Pantheon's wall. This mother of all domes would be redesigned several times before taking its final shape, with contributions by architects including Sangallo the Younger, Raphael, and Michelangelo. The hoped-for perfection was not quite achieved, though: cracks in the dome were patched up with binding chains in 18th century.

Reaching the Heights

Bramante was succeeded as chief architect of St. Peter's by Raphael (1483–1520), whose architectural career was as significant as his sublime fine art. Raphael collaborated closely with Antonio da Sangallo the Younger (1484–1546), who had studied in Rome under Bramante and whose best-known works display his mentor's influence.

Despite the outward similarities to Classical structures, the domes and cupolas, statuary, columns and ornamentation of the High Renaissance were altogether more elaborate than their ancient predecessors.

MANNERISM

The word "mannerism" comes from the Italian word *maniera*, "style" or "technique." It was first used in the mid-sixteenth century to refer to painters of a younger generation who were starting to abandon their elders' quiet, Classical correctness for a more adventurously exhibitionistic style.

STYLE FILE

Notable Features:
Classical forms taken to extremes of virtuosity;
Effects of exaggeration and even imbalance.

Major Influences:
Crisis of confidence following Charles V's sack of Rome in 1527;
Sense that the aims of the Renaissance had all now been achieved.

Where and When:
Italy; c. 1530–90.

BELOW: *Palazzio Senatorio detail, in Michelangelo's Piazza del Campidoglio, Rome.*

Over the Top?

"Mannerism" was not necessarily a term of approval: such self-conscious virtuosity was viewed with some suspicion. Michelangelo's Piazza del Campidoglio in Rome was typical, achieved with breathtaking beauty and jaw-dropping panache, but almost *too* brilliant in its execution. Where a High Renaissance architect would have worked to ensure that everything looked exactly right, Michelangelo played with proportions and created shapes to counteract the effect of perspective. The Piazza's Museo Capitolino, for example, is a work of utterly accomplished and yet unsettling architectural ambiguity. Its giant columns belong to a colossal, single-storied building, whereas the tiered columns between suggest a more compact creation.

Commissioned by the city authorities, Michelangelo laid out the whole trapezoidal piazza as a "frame" for the ancient equestrian statue of Marcus Aurelius. He did so with astonishing success, though for some this very enlistment of architecture in the service of sculpture may have underlined the feeling that Mannerism was about self-indulgence.

The Two-in-One Church

Andrea Palladio (1508–80) was later to become associated with an almost ostentatiously modest version of Neoclassicism (*see* pages 138–39), but in his own day he was famed for his Mannerist works. His *Il Redentore* church was built to thank God for Venice's deliverance from plague in 1575–76, but for all its pious intent, it has an air of trickery. It, too, is two buildings in one. The first, seen across the water, is a massive, squat structure set off by its lofty campanile and dominated by its dome; the second is defined by its elegant, Greek-templelike facades.

ABOVE: *Palladio's* Il Redentore *church, Venice.*

AGONY, ECSTASY, AND ARCHITECTURE

Had he never painted or sculpted, Michelangelo Buonarroti would still have his place in cultural history as one of the greatest architects who ever lived. Born in 1475, his gifts were apparent even in his teens. His most famous painting was perhaps the Sistine Chapel ceiling; his most celebrated sculpture, arguably the Pietà in St. Peter's, Rome—a Mannerist classic in its extravagant emotionality. Look up from this, and you see the light streaming in from Michelangelo's vast dome—in its own way just as exquisite.

TUDOR AND JACOBEAN

In England, Renaissance architecture is usually referred to as the Elizabethan (early) or Jacobean (later) style. Queen Elizabeth I, who reigned 1558–1603, was the last Tudor monarch, so that Tudor architecture, which straddles the medieval and Renaissance stylistically, encompasses the Elizabethan.

STYLE FILE

Notable Features:
Tudor: Timber frames, with wattle and daub, often black and white; Projecting upper stories;
Elizabethan: Renaissance styles with Flemish gables and curves.
Jacobean: Italian-style formality in designs.

Major Influences:
Medieval origins; Dutch, Flemish and Italian styles.

Where and When:
England, 16th and 17th centuries.

Beauty in Black and White

The system of construction known as half-timbering was of medieval origin, but reached its high point in Tudor England (1485–1603). A timber framework was filled in with "wattle and daub"—a mesh of inter-woven reeds or twigs, caulked with mud and plaster, and whitewashed over.

Function was made a feature in this style: the rough-cut wood frame was visible and generally painted to contrast with the filler. A style that now symbolizes "timeless" English-ness thus affords intriguing comparisons with Postmodern monuments like the Pompidou Center, Paris (*see* page 249), with its exoskel-eton of pipes and ducts: both scorn to conceal their status as artificial, built constructions.

ABOVE: *Hardwick Hall (1590s), designed by Robert Smythson.*
OPPOSITE: *Speke Hall (1530–98), near Liverpool, England.*
BELOW: *Knole House, Kent, a Jacobean landmark.*

CHIMNEYS

A surprisingly late invention, made as recently as the 14th century, the chimney still seemed innovative in Tudor times. The transition from a simple hole in the roof to a vertical shaft that sucked up smoke and fumes, had changed home life immeasurably for the better. It is no surprise, then, that Tudor and Jacobean architects should have made their chimney stacks such a feature: elaborately curved, even cork-screwing constructions of patterned brick.

Elizabeth to James

England's greatest Elizabethan buildings are grand mansions rather than the religious landmarks of Renaissance Italy; since Henry VIII had split with Rome, lavish places of worship were out of fashion. Stonemasons of the Low Countries (*see* pages 100–1) brought their gables and pointed curves, which were popular in Elizabethan homes.

The more formal lines of Mannerist Italy had begun to influence architects by the time of the Jacobean period, that of James I of England (James IV of Scotland), 1603–25.

THE BAROQUE

It was, perhaps, inevitable that Renaissance should lead to Reformation. Protestantism placed the thinking individual at the very center of religious faith. What did Catholicism, with its rules and hierarchies, have to offer the newly self-conscious, self-confident humanist? The Church launched a more passionate, intensely experienced Catholicism in its Counter Reformation.

An Aesthetic of Assault

The architectural expression of the Counter Reformation was the Baroque, a style that set the symmetries of Renaissance Classicism off against the wildest extravagances of ornamentation. Simple, barrel-vaulted ceilings were transformed by spectacular paintings; florid columns glowed in gold leaf and marble; plain facades were bedecked with pilasters and ornamental urns. Where the statues and stained glass of the Gothic cathedrals had offered scriptural instruction to the uneducated, these interiors ravished the senses and took the soul by storm.

OPPOSITE, ABOVE: *Nicola Salvi's Trevi Fountain (1732–51. with input from Bernini) and the facade of Palazzo Poli, Rome.*
RIGHT: *The early Baroque Chiesa del Gesù, Rome (1584, facade by Giacomo della Porta).*
OPPOSITE, BELOW: *Window detail, Catania University, Sicily.*

Palaces and Propaganda

So rich an architectural mixture was far too intoxicating to be left to the Church. The Baroque style was quickly taken up in the secular sphere. In France and central Europe, where unpopular monarchies were attempting the same sort of ideological fight-back as the Catholic Church, Baroque palaces magnified the mystique of the ruling dynasties. Though sometimes exuberantly ornamented, exterior facades were often comparatively restrained, though this beautiful simplicity only heightened the shock and awe that awaited the visitor within. Throughout the late seventeenth and early eighteenth centuries, the Baroque style continued to develop, with regional differences reflecting local traditions and conditions.

ENGLISH BAROQUE

The most important event in English architectural history during this period came in 1666, when the Great Fire of London left the capital a smoking ruin. More than 13,000 houses were lost, along with important financial and public buildings, eighty-seven churches, and the city's Gothic cathedral, St. Paul's.

Phoenix Rising from the Ashes

The Great Fire was a tragedy, of course, and yet a new generation of young architects were not slow in seizing the opportunity. Chief among these was Sir Christopher Wren, whose most famous monument was to be the new St. Paul's; he had been powerfully impressed by what he had seen of Baroque architecture in Rome. So much so, indeed, that his first design for St. Paul's—a vast, domed structure with a sweeping ambulatory—was rejected as being

ABOVE: *The Sheldonian Theatre (1664–69), by Sir Christopher Wren, is the main academic and ceremonial assembly hall of the University of Oxford; it features a central octagonal cupola.*
RIGHT: *Sir John Vanbrugh's Blenheim Palace (1705–24), near Oxford, with its plethora of pilasters and pillars.*

THE "PRIMITIVE"

Nicholas Hawksmoor, observed Sir John Vanbrugh, combined "two qualities that are not often joined, modesty and merit"; much the same might be said of his architecture. Born around 1661, he built handsome country houses, as well as academic buildings for Oxford University, but is best remembered for his great London churches (c. 1714–30). Though every one is radically different, they share a certain austerity, which may have stemmed from his personal theological preoccupation with what he saw as the Christian duty to recover the "primitive" principles of the early Church.

ABOVE: *Detail of the dome, a tower and the tympanum above the Great West Door at St. Paul's Cathedral, London. The fifth on this site, Sir Christopher Wren's edifice was built after the Great Fire of London.*

too similar to St. Peter's to pass muster in Protestant England. His revised plan was just as ambitious, but much more sober—this was to be a hallmark of the English Baroque, as observed in works by architects like Nicholas Hawksmoor, James Gibbs, and Sir John Vanbrugh. The English Baroque is as spectacular as its Continental equivalent, but tends to be chaster decoratively, its emphasis on elegance and dignity rather than on the riotous complexity seen elsewhere.

ROCOCO

Baroque was taken to new extremes in eighteenth-century France. It was called "Rococo," a name that, compounding two French words, *rocaille* ("small stone") and *coquille* ("seashell"), suggested the fanciful forms to which pebbles and shells were worn on a wave-swept beach.

Putting on a Show

Church and state were the Western world's two great patrons of architecture through much of modern history: in France, the Bourbon monarchy played a leading role. Louis XIV, the "Sun King" (reigned 1643–1715), and his successors claimed an absolute authority over their subjects, which they underlined with a show of splendor. From 1661, architect Louis le Vau worked with landscape designer André Le Nôtre to create a fitting showcase for French royalty at Versailles. No one approaching the new palace through its magnificent grounds could doubt the divine right of the king to rule: the message was implicit, yet unmistakable.

ABOVE: *Decadent marble and gilded ornamentation at the Palace of Versailles, France.*
RIGHT: *The Elector's Palace at Trier, Germany, is replete with putti, swags, and statuettes.*

Up close the Rococo was as overwhelming, but a great deal more lighthearted: a luxuriant outpouring of swirling shell shapes and foliate flourishes. Unabashedly frivolous, Rococo buildings often had the look of being created of confectioner's sugar, the architectural equivalents of the paintings of Watteau and Fragonard .

ABOVE: *The grounds and main courtyard entrance at Zwinger Palace, Dresden, Germany.*

An Aesthetic for Export

From France, Rococo spread quickly; it was not exclusively an architectural style, but a movement in interior decor, painting, and furniture design. As such, its influence was communicated not only by French artists, but by objects, and was adopted enthusiastically elsewhere. In England, "the French taste," as it was disdainfully called, was never much more than a minor fad, but in Catholic southern Germany and Austria it fitted well with the Baroque sensibility then prevailing.

Rococo fell from favor with a post-Romantic sensibility that saw no distinction between the decorative and the decadent, but our "Postmodern" age has rediscovered the joys of parody and playfulness, the pleasures of the Rococo style (*see* page 252).

READY FOR ROCOCO

The Zwinger Palace, in Dresden, Germany, was built between 1722 and 1733 to a design by Matthäus Daniel Pöppelmann. It was commissioned by Augustus II, King of Poland and Elector of Saxony, who wanted a palace complex similar to the Forum in Rome. But, though grouped around an esplanade and very distantly Classical in its broad symmetries, the result would hardly have been recognized by Cicero or Caesar. For, while not as fluffy as French Rococo, the Zwinger's style shows all the late-Baroque exuberance that was to make Germany so receptive to the new aesthetic.

ALPINE AND BOHEMIAN

A massive mountain range straddling central Europe, the Alps extend across France, Italy, Austria, Slovenia, Liechtenstein, Germany, and Switzerland; Bohemia lies just to the east. It is no surprise to find that so unique an environment should have an architectural tradition all its own.

STYLE FILE

Notable Features:
Steeply pitched roofs; Wood-built, wide-eaved chalet cabins in the mountainous terrain, but wider range of architecture in valleys.

Major Influences:
Traditional chalet design to suit winter weather; Baroque styles.

Where and When:
Alpine region, Moravia and Czech Republic; 16th–18th centuries.

Architectural Emblem

The traditional mountain herder's cottage or chalet (often called the "Swiss chalet"), built of wood, with widely overhanging eaves and practical window shutters, is to be found with minor variations in Bohemia and throughout the Alpine region. Such dwellings had come to symbolize the Alpine region even before the style was taken up enthusiastically by the twentieth-century tourist industry, which enjoyed a boom when skiing became popular in the postwar period. It is appropriate enough in some respects, but it may give a misleading impression, for there is a great deal more to the Alpine region than its mountains.

Barrier or Crossroads?

If the Alps were a formidable barrier, their valleys and passes were a vital thoroughfare: all overland trade and travel between Italy and northern Europe passed through these valleys, while Bohemia (largely, today's Czech Republic) was a communications crossroads. This left architectural traces that may still be seen today. Always predominantly Catholic (and the Alps abutting Italy geographically), the region has a particularly splendid heritage of attractive Baroque architecture.

ABOVE, LEFT: A traditional mountainside chalet in Austria.
ABOVE: Window shutters and paintwork detail on a classic Swiss chalet.

ECLECTIC INNSBRUCK

The Austrian city of Innsbruck is on the contemporary architectural map, thanks to its city hall (Dominique Perrault, 2002), but it also boasts a fine collection of older architecture. Numerous monuments in the Gothic, Renaissance, and Baroque styles testify to the city's commercial—and cultural—enrichment through several centuries of trade.

LEFT: Baroque towers on the castle and a church and a mixture of Gothic and Baroque houses in Cesky Krumlov, a walled city of 14th- to 17th-century buildings near the Czech–Austrian border.
OPPOSITE: Baroque domes in the skyline of Salzburg, Austria.

SPANISH BAROQUE

By the seventeenth century, Spain already had a long and distinguished architectural history. It could boast some of Europe's oldest Romanesque architecture, as well as great Gothic cathedrals like Burgos, Toledo, and León. The great Islamic monuments of al-Andalus (*see* page 44) were also part of its heritage, even if they were preserved mainly for the propagandistic purpose of underscoring the success of the Christian *reconquista* ("reconquest") of the country.

The "Golden Age"

Spain's discoveries and conquests in the Americas brought a sixteenth- and seventeenth-century "Golden Age" (*Siglo de Oro*), which corresponded with the Counter Reformation and the Baroque. Spain's monarchs took a leading role in promoting Catholicism and suppressing heresy, and that purist fervor is evident in the art and architecture of the time.

As golden ages go, Spain's was a remarkably austere, even gloomy, one: think of the paintings of El Greco—despite their wild mannerism, fundamentally simple—for example. Philip II's great palace complex, San Lorenzo de El Escorial (late sixteenth century), is

CHEERFUL CHURRIGUERA

So much severity would have been hard to bear had it not been for the very different Baroque spirit introduced into Spain by José Bonito Churriguera (1665–1725) and his followers. Churriguera's energetic, mesmerizingly ornate, yet at the same time dynamic and fluid style is now known as the "Churrigueresque." Despite its name, it would reach its zenith after its originator's death, in the main facade of Murcia Cathedral (1730s).

almost aggressively plain in its design. Part-palace, part-monastery, part-mausoleum for himself and for all the monarchs of Spain, this vast monument was designed by Juan de Herrera. Its beauty is chaste and intimidating; the only concession that Herrera and the king allowed themselves was to arrange the complex on a gridlike ground plan in honor of the grid on which St. Lawrence was martyred.

TOP LEFT: *Churrigueresque columns, or* estipiti, *at the church in Caravaca de la Cruz.*
TOP: *Granada Cathedral detail.*
OPPOSITE: *El Escorial, a palace and monastery near Madrid, designed by Juan de Herrera.*
LEFT: *The Churrigueresque facade of the Romanesque cathedral at Santiago de Compostela (see also page 33).*

MEDITERRANEAN STYLES

A clear continuity can be seen to exist between the traditional domestic architecture of southern Europe and the forms that are known to have been used in the Greek and Roman worlds in Classical times.

STYLE FILE

Notable Features:
Simple, boxy construction;
Roofs often flat, given
 sparsity of rain;
Outside walls white-
 washed, or painted in
 pastel shades.

Major Influences:
Ancient traditions
 enduring, despite other
 decorative influences.

Where and When:
Smaller towns and
 villages of Portugal and
 the coastal regions of
 Mediterranean countries;
 16th–18th centuries.

Public vs. Private

Greek and Roman men of note, we know, spent much of their time in public spaces, talking with friends in the *agora* or *forum*, for instance, or addressing the various political assemblies. At day's end, though, they withdrew into the secluded space of the family home. Well-born women were virtual prisoners here, in houses that opened inward upon airy courtyards, but cold-shouldered the outside world with their blank and windowless external walls. A similar opposition has endured into modern times in many of the villages and small towns of southern Europe, social life taking place in the street, with its markets, bars, and pavement cafés, while the privacy of the home itself is sacrosanct.

RIGHT: *Elaborate sixteenth-century ornamentation in Portugal is known as Manueline (for Manuel I, reign 1495–1521).* BELOW: *A bell tower atop a simple church on the Greek island of Patmos.*

Whiter than White

This division is embodied architecturally in the traditional Mediterranean dwelling—at its simplest no more than a box built of mud brick, or in later times, of stone. A dazzling coat of simple whitewash reflected the worst of the sun, but served a symbolic purpose, too, anthropologists say, in representing the inviolable purity of the family inside.

Larger houses might have more pretensions, with clear nods in the direction of the Baroque—this is true, too, of the more prestigious public buildings and churches. For the most part, though, wider trends in architecture had to take second place to age-old anxieties about the sanctity of the family.

ABOVE: *Simple, boxy, whitewashed cottages in a typical Portuguese village.*

BELOW: *Pastels, whites, and simple curves and domes in a picture-postcard scene on a sun-drenched Greek island.*

ON THE HOUSE IN GREECE

The Greek word *oikos* or "house" had a quasi-sacred significance and embraced not just the built structure of the dwelling, but the family within it—as well as all of the ancestors. Not only did the household have to be sheltered and physically protected from the elements and the outside world, but its honor had to be upheld—through acts of vengeance or generations of blood feud if need be.

THE LOW COUNTRIES

The seventeenth century saw the Low Countries coming into their own. Flanders (the far northeast of France and Belgium), though a possession of Spain, was nevertheless flourishing. To the north, the United Provinces (Holland) had gained their independence and acquired a new national identity.

The Work Ethic

The new nation prospered, thanks to its industrious farmers, weavers, and craftsmen, and the Dutch navigators opening up an empire in the Indies and beyond. The country's economic miracle was driven not by the aristocracy, but by wealthy magnates and honest burghers; the newly formed society had quickly rejected Spanish-style Catholicism for Lutheran Protestantism in all its stark simplicities. In architecture, accordingly, the Dutch achievement is most typically to be seen not in the princely palace or spectacular cathedral, but in the merchant's townhouse, handsome, yet sober and unassuming.

Those of Amsterdam are justly famous: hundreds throng the banks of the Amstel River

ABOVE: *Baroque facades in Amsterdam's Begijnhof court.*
OPPOSITE: *Baroque guildhalls (1690s) on the Grand Place in Brussels, Belgium.*
BELOW: *Late sixteenth-century guild houses by Hans Vredeman, the best-known Flemish Baroque architect, Grote Markt, Antwerp, Belgium.*

and surrounding canals, their narrow facades rising high toward the sky. Pulleys above their topmost windows tend to lend a workmanlike air: in many cases merchants would actually have used the lower stories of their homes for warehousing goods. Besides, so narrow were the staircases and passages in buildings with such a narrow frontage that it made sense to lift larger items of furniture up and bring them into the house via open windows.

GREAT GABLES

The architectural ideal for the Netherlands' merchant elite was one of neatness and good order: ostentation was frowned upon. Town-houses could be adorned discreetly with patterned brickwork and the shapely pointed gables. These were most frequently stepped, though narrow, straight-sided "neck gables"—which featured ornamental scrolling—were also widely used.

RUSSIAN BAROQUE

By the beginning of the sixteenth century, the country we now know as Russia was starting to take shape around the ever-growing power of the principality of Muscovy. Gradually, an architectural tradition molded largely by Byzantine influences (*see* pages 30–31) gave way to a new and distinctive Russian style.

STYLE FILE

Notable Features:
Early Byzantine forms giving way to local forms (tent roofs, onion domes, spires);
Extravagant Baroque from 17th century;
"Rastrelliesque" Baroque prevailed in 18th century.

Major Influences:
Byzantine to begin with;
Local developments responded mainly to practical problems;
Versions of Baroque introduced from West from 17th century.

Where and When:
Russia, Ukraine;
16th–18th centuries.

Muscovite Baroque

Remote though they were from the West, dwellers in the Russian interior had long traded downriver with the Byzantine Empire. Having embraced the Orthodox religion, it was only natural that they should have absorbed the orthodox architectural principles of Byzantium, too; that they did is clear from many of the churches of the time.

The environment here was very different, though: for one thing, timber abounded in Russia's forests, a fact reflected not just in domestic, but in ecclesiastical architecture. Brick was also used; by the sixteenth century the tented roof had been introduced for both wood- and brick-built churches. Roughly conical, it prevented accumulations of heavy snow. For the same reason, innovations were made to the design of the centerpiece of any

OPPOSITE, TOP: *The famous spires and domes of St. Basil's Cathedral, Moscow.*

RIGHT: *Detail of the cathedral at Novodevichy (New Maidens') Convent, Smolensk. Built in the seventeenth century, it remained intact during the entire era of Soviet communism.*

OPPOSITE, BELOW: *Facade detail of Rastrelli's Catherine Palace (1752–56), St. Petersburg.*

Byzantine church, the dome: small, steep-sided "helmet domes" and bulbous "onion spires" were both introduced around this time, while in the Ukraine, so-called "pear domes" served the same purpose.

Naryshkin and Rastrelli

By the end of the seventeenth century, Russia's rulers were embracing the Baroque, whose influence had come to Russia via the Ukraine. A distinctive hybrid style arose, known as Naryshkin Baroque after the aristo-crat who first used it to build highly orna-mented chapels on his estate. Soon Russian architecture seemed to be disappearing beneath a tide of decoration. In the eigh-teenth century, a purer Baroque was intro-duced to Russia by the Italian-born architect Bartolomeo Rastrelli; his most famous monu-ments include the Winter Palace (1753).

THE
NEW WORLD

When European settlers first began to make their way into North and South America and other colonial outposts, bringing with them their own building techniques and aesthetics, they found that they had to adapt these to meet the needs of survival in their new environment, which often had a climate and a supply of raw materials that was very different from what they had left behind. The settlers also found that their "new" world was already populated by nations of native peoples who had their own construction styles tailored to their surroundings. As time passed, and as settlers and indigenous peoples borrowed and adapted knowledge from each other, new forms and styles evolved.

OPPOSITE: *This simple, but serviceable, log cabin was home to a frontier family: Pfeiffer's Homestead, Grand Teton National Park, Wyoming.*

PRE–COLUMBIAN

At least 3,000 years before Europeans reached the New World, the native peoples of South and Central America designed and built houses, public buildings, and temples that reflect their own lifeways, surroundings, and techniques.

STYLE FILE

Notable Features:
Organic matter or stone
  construction;
Post-and-lintel system;
Corbeled arches (Chavín
  and Mayan peoples);
Pyramids and temples;
Carved adornments,
  mostly featuring animals.

Major Influences:
Ancient traditions;
Local environmental
  factors.

Where and When:
South and Central
  America;
c. 1500 BC–AD 1540.

BELOW: *Stepped pyramid at Chichen Itzá, Yucatán.*

Materials and Methods

Some of the earliest-known pre-Columbian buildings were constructed from organic materials such as wood, bundled reeds, fiber matting, and thatch. The settled peoples of Mesoamerica and the central Andean area developed a more permanent architecture using stone and adobe (sun-dried bricks or plaster). Most structures were built using a simple post-and-lintel, or horizontal-beam, system, although the Chavín of Peru and the Maya of Mesoamerica used a corbeled, or "false," arch (in which stones are placed upon one another to form an archlike shape).

Pre-Columbian Pyramids

Using stone tools and human labor, the peoples of ancient Mesoamerica constructed great pyramids that were used as religious

temples, tombs, and for military defense. Tellingly, the Aztec symbol for conquest was a burning pyramid in which the temple surmounting it (called a *calli*) had been toppled. Whenever a new leader came to power, or when one group was vanquished by another, it was not uncommon for Meso-american pyramids to be rebuilt over the pre-existing structures, in order to make them more favorable to the new rulers.

ABOVE: *Animal-head carving detail at Chichen Itzá.*
BELOW: *The famous "false" arch at the Great Palace of Labná, Yucatán, Mexico.*

PUEBLO/ADOBE

Adobe—a mixture of mud, water, and straw or other fibrous material dried in the sun—is among the oldest materials used for construction on the North American continent. It is widely seen in the American Southwest.

An Ancient Tradition

The basic structure of the Pueblo building—with earthen walls and a flat roof—was first developed more than 1,000 years ago by the Native American inhabitants of what are now New Mexico and Arizona. They built simple, large, multifamily dwellings with stepped or terraced levels (which the Spanish colonists called "pueblos," meaning "villages"), using ladders to move between levels. The adobe was made by puddling mud with straw and building this up in layers, allowing successive layers to dry before applying more mud. Finished walls were regularly renewed with fresh layers of mud. The distinguishing characteristics of multilevel Pueblo buildings include thick adobe walls with rounded corners, flat roofs, and small windows.

ABOVE: *Santa Fe, New Mexico's, Palace of the Governors.*
OPPOSITE: *Taos Pueblo, New Mexico.*

TAOS PUEBLO

Taos Pueblo is the longest continuously inhabited community in the United States. This massive structure consists of two groups of houses with terraced upper levels. The upper units are accessed by ladders through holes in the roofs. The outer and upper rooms serve as the living quarters, while those deeper within the pueblo are used for storage. The dwellings are renovated annually in a village ceremony in which the walls are refinished with a new coat of adobe plaster.

Spanish Adaptation

During the seventeenth and eighteenth centuries, Spanish colonists in the Southwest adapted the Pueblo construction materials and techniques to suit their own needs. They formed the adobe into sun-dried bricks (the word "adobe" is derived from the Arabic *atob*, meaning "brick"), which they stacked and mortared with mud and then covered with protective layers of adobe. The Spanish used metal tools that made it easier to cut the timber that they needed for the supporting roof rafters (vigas) and ceiling poles (latillas).

Environmentally Friendly

Pueblo Revival homes have been popular since the early twentieth century. Thick adobe walls absorb heat during the day and radiate it slowly as the air cools. With their shady interiors, these homes are environmentally friendly, and their rough-hewn, hand-crafted look has helped fuel the renewed popularity of this style in the Southwest today.

SPANISH MISSION

The historic missions of the American Southwest were founded in the eighteenth century by Dominican, Jesuit, and Franciscan missionaries from Spain and built with indigenous labor. Combining local materials and techniques with Spanish Baroque architecture from the Old World, a unique style was created.

STYLE FILE

Notable Features:
Thick, adobe-brick walls;
Rounded corners;
Flat roofs;
Arches and domes;
Small, rounded windows;
Decorative facade gables;
Prominent belfries;
Symmetrical facades;
Niches in church walls
  (for religious statuary).

Major Influences:
Pueblo/Adobe;
Spanish Baroque.

Where and When:
Florida, c. 1550s–1750;
Southwest, 18th century.

Self-supporting Communities

The Spanish missions were built as isolated, self-sustaining communities in which religious conversion of the native people was a priority, but raising crops and livestock was also a necessity. The typical mission consisted of a large central quadrangle, usually with a fountain at its center, surrounded by grain storage and living quarters in the cool interiors that were created by the thick, adobe-brick walls. The bricks were cemented with crushed limestone mortar, leaving small (or no) window openings. The church would have a tall bell tower and beautiful (if simple) ornamentation, either of carvings or frescoes. In California, twenty-one such communities were built (the first, Mission San Diego de Alcalá, was founded in 1769).

RIGHT: *The Mission of San Antonio de Padua was founded in what is now Texas by Franciscan missionaries in 1744. The building was later used as a fort and is better known as the Alamo.*

OPPOSITE: *The simple, adobe mission church at Rancho de Taos, New Mexico, was made famous by Ansel Adams and Georgia O'Keeffe, among other artists. Its construction mirrors indigenous Pueblo styles.*

Old World Influences

The missions of Florida, the earliest being in St. Augustine (founded 1565), feature graceful curvilinear gables that are usually flanked by twin belfries; ornate sculptures above the entrances and windows; and grand arched portals. Domes and vaulted ceilings are usually found in such churches, many of which were built in the eighteenth century on sites established much earlier. They resemble Spanish Baroque buildings and were less influenced by local tradition than the missions of the Southwest. But in both regions, the influence of Moorish architecture is also seen in the use of interior arches and/or colonnaded courtyards. The sculpted portals and window details on many mission buildings display the Spanish preference for elaborate masonry carvings decorating otherwise plain wall surfaces, though sometimes frescoes were painted instead. Mexican or European artisans were employed by the missionaries to emulate the lavish, opulent buildings of Spain.

MEN WITH A MISSION

Known as the "Mother of Missions," the first one in California was Mission San Diego de Alcalá, founded in 1769 by Father Junipero Serra. The church that can be seen today dates from 1813 (below, during its 1930s restoration). By the time this building was erected, 6 miles inland from the original site, Mission San Diego had survived calamities including riots, fire, and two earthquakes.

ENGLISH COLONIAL

In the seventeenth century, Puritan settlers brought to America a rural English architecture that was largely late medieval in form and detail, which they adapted for their new environment. Their mainly wooden homes were modest, simple, and straightforward, with minimal decoration, as the Puritans considered ornamentation to be a sign of vanity.

STYLE FILE

Notable Features:
Timber construction;
Exposed trusses;
Gabled, steep roofs;
Clapboard siding or
  weathered shingles;
Large, central chimney;
Symmetrical facades;
Casement windows.

Major Influences:
English medieval;
Puritan austerity.

Where and When:
Mainly New England and
  Mid-Atlantic region;
  c.1620–1850.

Planned Communities

Though they had left English villages that had developed slowly and organically over hundreds of years, the merchants and farmers who settled the New World had to build their new communities all at once, quickly and efficiently. They organized their villages with the houses clustered around a green or "common," with a religious meetinghouse that also served as the community center. The settlers constructed their homes using familiar methods, making adaptations as required. Instead of building stone dwellings, like those they had left behind, they used the wood that was plentiful in the New England forests to construct two-story boxlike dwellings that were

DEERFIELD VILLAGE

More than 300 years old, the historic village of Old Deerfield is now a living museum of rural, colonial Massachusetts. The village was raided by French and Indian warriors in 1704 and largely burned to the ground, but was subsequently rebuilt. Today, thirteen restored houses, built between 1730 and 1850, provide one of the best opportunities anywhere to see authentic English Colonial architecture.

usually two rooms wide and one or two rooms deep. Some of these homes were built with a second-story overhang or jetty, to create more space. They covered the heavy oak frames with unpainted clapboard or shingle siding, to provide protection from the harsh New England winters. The shingled roofs were steeply pitched so as to shed the heavy snowfall; a massive chimney was centrally placed for optimal warmth, and they constructed heavy doors and small casement windows.

Variations

The most readily recognizable form of the New England Colonial style is the Saltbox house (*see* overleaf). Larger and more grandiose brick or stone versions of the English Colonial home were built by wealthier colonists. In the more southern English colonies around the Chesapeake Bay and in the Carolinas, the first settlers constructed wooden homes with structural posts that were placed directly in the ground. As a result, these dwellings fell easily to rot and termites, and no examples remain.

SALTBOX HOUSES

This distinctive English Colonial style is most often found in New England, where it became highly popular between 1680 and 1830 for its practical, sloping, lean-to gable roofline, which was particularly useful for shedding heavy snow. It takes its name from a type of wooden box that was used to store salt.

STYLE FILE

Notable Features:
Timber construction;
Sloping lean-to;
Gable roof with extended
  rear slope;
Clapboard siding or
  weathered shingles;
Large, central chimney;
Casement windows;
Pendants;
May have overhanging
  second story, or jetty.

Major Influences:
English medieval.

Where and When:
Mainly New England,
  c. 1650–1850.

Adding Space

Early English Colonial homes were often only a single room deep, which meant close living quarters for the colonists, who might have lived in households of a dozen or more people. When more room was needed to accommodate their expanding families, the addition of sapce at the rear provided extra rooms. The typical English Colonial dwelling was adapted to the Saltbox style by the addition of a one-story lean-to across the rear of a one-and-one-half- or two-story structure, which provided extra rooms and extended the rear slope of the gable roof, forming the classic "saltbox" shape. In most Saltbox homes, the rear addition was divided into three rooms: a central kitchen, a pantry, and a further room.

STANLEY-WHITMAN HOUSE

Location: Farmington, Connecticut.
Date: 1720.
Materials: Timber; stone chimney.
Significance: This is one of the best-known examples of English Colonial architecture. It features an overhanging second story with pendants and diamond-paned sash windows, a large central chimney, and a lean-to (giving it the traditional Saltbox shape). A National Historic Landmark, the restored building is now a museum.

ABOVE: *The Stanley-Whitman House, Connecticut.*

OPPOSITE: *A Deerfield Saltbox in wintry conditions.*

BELOW: *This c.1700 Saltbox has an asymmetrical frontage.*

Deciphering History

Some Saltbox houses show a clear break in the roofline, indicating that the lean-to was added as a later addition to the structure. However, the lack of a break in the roofline of a Saltbox home does not necessarily mean that the lean-to was part of the original house, as it was a common practice to alter the original roofline at the time of the addition in order to provide adequate ceiling space for the new rooms.

PENNSYLVANIA DUTCH

This style is named for the Pennsylvania Dutch people, including the Mennonites and the Amish, who left Switzerland and Germany for religious freedom. "Dutch" is a corruption of *Deutsch*, meaning "German"—and both German and Swiss building techniques were used in Pennsylvania.

STYLE FILE

Notable Features:
Masonry construction or
 foundations;
Timber frameworks;
Stone chimneys;
Raised wood paneling;
Sash windows;
Dormers and double
 "Dutch" doorways.

Major Influences:
German and Alpine
 vernacular styles.

Where and When:
Pennsylvania and the
 Northeast; c. 1700
 onward.

Farmhouse Architecture

The Pennsylvania Dutch settlers were farmers, and their rustic farmsteads were simple and functional. Distinguishing characteristics include a broad roof, sometimes gambrel or with flaring eaves, double-hung sash windows, dormers, end walls of stone, raised wood paneling, and a chimney located at one or both ends. A central double "Dutch" doorway is divided horizontally—this was once used to keep livestock out of the home while allowing light and air in through the open top. Early examples were generally combined farm/barns. These houses are often "banked" into a hillside, thereby providing warmth in the winter and coolness in the summer.

ABOVE: *A banked barn, adorned with colorful hex signs, in Lehigh County, Pennsylvania.*
OPPOSITE: *The beautifully preserved Hans Herr House in Lancaster County.*
BELOW: *This heavy-masonry Pennsylvania Dutch building has Alpine shutters at the ground level.*

HANS HERR HOUSE

Location: Lancaster County, Pennsylvania.
Date: 1719.
Materials: Uncoursed sandstone.
Significance: This is the oldest building in Lancaster County and the oldest Mennonite meeting place in North America. Now part of a museum, which also includes farmhouses and outbuildings, the complex as a whole boasts perhaps the best extant examples of the Pennsylvania Dutch style.

Colorful Legacy

There has been much scholarly debate over the origin and the meaning of so-called "hex signs," the colorful symbols used as decoration by the Pennsylvania Dutch. According to some, these symbols were painted onto barns in order to keep evil spirits away or to bring good luck (*Hexe* is the German word for "witch"). However, the most common hex signs are six-sided geometric figures, and the German word for "six" is *sechs*, which may have evolved into "hex." Whatever their origin, hex signs have come to be associated with the distinctive culture of these settlers.

SHAKER ARCHITECTURE

The Shakers began as a communitarian religious group that splintered from a Quaker community in England and sought religious freedom in the New World. They followed a simpler, less hierarchical lifestyle than other groups, and the houses they built and the communities they lived in reflected this.

Utopian Ideals

The Shakers were named for their ecstatic, trancelike liturgical dances (they were also called "Shaking Quakers"). Among other things, they were committed to celibate communal living—and, along with their Utopian ideals, they brought a new type of architecture to the American landscape. The Shakers sought simplicity and perfection in all things, including their work and their surroundings.

Simplicity and Utility

The Shakers embodied the virtues of simplicity and utility, and they handcrafted plain and simple dwellings and furnishings of natural materials. Superfluity of any kind—carvings, veneers, cornices, or ornamentation—was to them a vulgar symbol of pride and dishonesty.

Defining Characteristics

Shaker communities generally consisted of functional farmhouses and outbuildings, with a centrally located meetinghouse. To allow for minimal contact between the sexes, the typical dwelling had two entrance doors, two stairwells, and separate hallways leading to the sleeping chambers. There was a common dining room, though men and women ate at separate tables. The meetinghouses often had three entrance doors: one for the men, one for the women, and one for the ministry. Door and window frames, lintels, chimneys, stairways, and other features were all produced in their most basic form, with clean lines and no frills. Interiors were sparse and clean, with open floor spaces to accommodate religious dances; because of the open interiors, the buildings required a large truss to support the roof. To save space, the carpenters built drawers and closets into the walls, and rows of pegboards (at about 6 feet high, for hanging chairs when not in use) were built into almost every room. Of primary concern in Shaker housing construction were good lighting, heating, and ventilation.

ABOVE: *The family dwelling house (1793) at Canterbury Shaker Village, New Hampshire.*
OPPOSITE: *Simple barns at Sabbathday Lake.*
BELOW: *Round barn at Hancock Shaker Village, Massachusetts.*

SABBATHDAY LAKE

The Sabbathday Lake Community in New Gloucester, Maine, is the last remaining active Shaker community. The meetinghouse (1794), the primary place of worship, is the only intact, first-generation Shaker meetinghouse in its original location. Public meeting (worship) services are still held here each Sunday.

FRENCH COLONIAL: ACADIA

The first Europeans to inhabit Canada were French fur traders, who had set up year-round settlements by the early 1600s. In building their first colonies, they were primarily concerned with defense—against both the Native Americans and the English. Thus, the early French settlement at Quebec City was dominated by a large fortress and defensive outer walls.

New France

In the early 1700s, the official territory of New France extended from Newfoundland to Lake Superior and from the Hudson Bay to the Gulf of Mexico. In the north, including eastern Canada and New England, the earliest French settlers built simple dwellings of wood or timber frames infilled with stones and mortar. Wood and stone farmhouses dotted the banks of the St. Lawrence River. They were typically low and rectangular, with steeply pitched roofs, and were clad with stucco or wooden planks, resembling farmhouses in Normandy, a rural area of northern France. In New England and rural eastern Canada, they built farmsteads with connected barns, flared roofs, and open courtyards.

TOP: *A French farmhouse in rural Canada, with its distinctive, steep roof shape.*
OPPOSITE, ABOVE: *A simple cottage in the French style, with a flared roof, in rural Quebec.*
RIGHT: *A colonial stone house.*
OPPOSITE, BELOW: *A Montreal stone townhouse.*

Stone Houses

A fire in Montreal in 1721 led to a 1727 ordinance that encouraged fire-resistant construction, after which time the residents of Montreal (and other major towns) began to build their houses of stone, with the fireplaces and chimneys built into the outside walls. To serve as firebreaks, interior walls extended through the roofs.

ACADIA

In 1605, French traders established the first of the five colonies of New France. Located chiefly in what is now Nova Scotia, it extended south as far as Maine. The territory was much contested between the French and the English, until 1713, when the English finally gained control. During the French and Indian War (1755–63), many Acadians were expelled (a large number fleeing south to Louisiana, where they became known as Cajuns). Meanwhile, Scots settlers moved in, and the area became known as Nova Scotia.

Stately Structures

In Quebec City, institutional buildings were mostly constructed in four units, two or three stories high, arranged around a square, open courtyard. Their walls were of mortared stone rubble, with arched windows and a sloped roof of tin tiles (*ferblanc*) with dormers. The homes of the wealthy resembled those of Paris, having a high central block flanked by two wings and with a gated courtyard in front. These homes were sometimes given Classical details like columns, pilasters, and pediments over windows and doorways.

DUTCH COLONIAL

In the early 1600s, Dutch and Huguenot settlers sailed to America in search of religious tolerance in the New World. They set up their trading colonies around the Hudson and Delaware Rivers, building their homes in the Dutch style, of stone and wood, or, in urban areas, of brick laid in Dutch patterns.

STYLE FILE

Notable Features:
Gambrel roof, steeply
  pitched with wide
  overhangs and flared
  eaves;
Straight-sided gables
  finished with parapets
  raised on elbows;
Dutch cross-bond
  pattern in bricklaying;
Iron anchor beams;
Double-hung windows,
  in gable or gambrel end;
Board-and-batten shutters;
Wide horizontal boards;
Front stoop;
Gable-end chimney;
Divided "Dutch" doors.

Major Influences:
Dutch vernacular styles.

Where and When:
The "Middle Colonies"
  (New York, New Jersey,
  Delaware, Pennsylvania);
  c. 1625–1840 (1900s,
  Revival).

The Signature Gambrel Roof

The typical Dutch Colonial home was surmounted by a steeply pitched gambrel roof—having two slopes, with the lower (steeper) slope often flared out in front of and behind the house to form an overhang, providing shelter from the rain. The straight-sided gables were finished with parapets raised on elbows.

Dutch Colonial Town Homes

Dutch Colonial townhouses were generally four or five stories tall, with the owner and his family living in the upper stories, above the street-level store. Bricks were usually laid in the Dutch cross-bond pattern. The front door was often divided horizontally, so that light and air could be admitted through the upper part, while roaming animals would be kept out. Examples of these can still be seen in New Jersey's Bergen and Rockland counties and in the Hudson Valley and Brooklyn, Queens, and Staten Island, New York.

ABOVE: *A rural Dutch Colonial–style farmhouse, a building style still seen widely in New York's Hudson Valley.*

Later Variants

Dutch Colonial–style elements are sometimes seen combined with Georgian details, such as dormer windows. In the early twentieth century, the Dutch Colonial style enjoyed a revival in the American suburbs. These Dutch Colonial Revival homes were designed with varying degrees of faithfulness to the original style, generally having symmetrical facades and doorways ornamented with columns, sidelights, and transoms.

ABOVE: *A Dutch Colonial home at Toddsbury, Virginia.*

BELOW: *The Old Manse, Concord, Massachusetts.*

THE OLD MANSE

Location: Concord, Massachusetts.
Date: c. 1770.
Architect: The Reverend William Emerson.
Significance: The Manse is situated along the Concord River, near the North Bridge, the site of the first organized armed resistance of the Revolutionary War. It was built by the grandfather of Ralph Waldo Emerson. Nathaniel Hawthorne honeymooned here, and he named the house in 1846 with the publication of his short-story collection *Mosses from an Old Manse.*

FRENCH COLONIAL: CREOLE AND THE SOUTH

The word "Creole" refers to the mixed heritage of the settlers of the Gulf Coast around Louisiana—primarily descended from French settlers, but their heritage also includes Spanish, African, and Native American influences. French Creole architecture contains elements borrowed from all these cultures: the settlers adapted their knowledge of construction to build dwellings that were suited to the damp, hot climate of the South.

STYLE FILE

Notable Features:
High, steeply pitched, hipped or pavilion-type roof, with the lower slope projecting out to form the porch cover;
Half-timber framing (called "post on sill" or *poteaux-sur-sole*), infilled with brick or *bousillage* (mud, moss, and animal hair);
Raised living quarters;
Narrow dormer windows;
Double French doors and casement windows;
Full-length porches (often two-storied);
No interior hallways;
Large, stone chimneys;
Stucco siding, or hand-split or riven shingles;
Raised basement;
Stuccoed brick or thin wooden columns;
Exterior staircase.

Major Influences:
Rural French, Neoclassical, and Caribbean.

Where and When:
Louisiana, Mississippi, Missouri, and Illinois; c. 1700–1830.

The Basic Model

The Creole homes of Louisiana, Mississippi, Missouri, and Illinois were simple, rectangular, stucco-sided dwellings that were one or two stories high and two to four rooms wide. They were built of brick and bald cypress (which was strong, pliable, and resistant to rot). These homes had full-length, two-story porches that served as passageways, since there were no interior hallways (to eliminate spaces lacking fresh air flow). The steeply pitched, hipped roofs extended outward beyond the walls to form galleries on the sides of the houses. Other defining features included casement windows, shutters, double French doors, and transoms; lacy ironwork trim was a later addition to wealthier homes.

RIGHT: *A Louisiana raised cottage, with a brick lower story.*

Louisiana Raised Cottages

Because of seasonal flooding and the dampness of the new environment, the colonists preferred to build their homes with the living space one story above the ground—creating a raised masonry basement, with a dirt or brick floor, that was used mainly for storage. This is known as the Louisiana raised cottage.

Farmsteads

A typical Creole farm had separate outbuildings used as kitchens, for livestock of various kinds, and *garçonnières* (for the young men to socialize in), all of which were located near the main house. High ceilings, 10 to 22 feet, in the main house allowed for tall windows and doors, which, like the exterior passageways, were devised to increase air flow.

ABOVE: *Facade detail of historic Elmscourt, near Natchez, Mississippi.*

HOMEPLACE PLANTATION

Location: Hahnville, Louisiana.
Date: 1787–91.
Materials: Cypress timbers infilled with clay and Spanish moss; brick.
Significance: This National Historic Landmark, located on the west bank of the Mississippi River, is one of the best-preserved examples of a large French Creole raised cottage.

AFRICAN INFLUENCES

When Africans were brought to the Americas as slaves in the seventeenth and eighteenth centuries, they brought with them a varied and rich heritage of language, cuisine, music, song and dance, religious practices, art, and architecture, which was preserved despite suppression, and whose legacy continues today.

STYLE FILE

Notable Features:
Hipped roof;
Oversized, overhanging
  eaves;
Linear, "shotgun" layout;
Front porch;
Thatched roof (now
  obsolete).

Major Influences:
African vernacular.

Where and When:
The American South;
  c. 17th century onward.

OPPOSITE, BELOW: *The African House at Melrose (formerly Yucca) Plantation, Louisiana.*
BELOW: *An African-influenced house in Georgia, with a hipped roof, overhanging eaves, and large porch.*

Slave Houses

Colonial slave houses of the South were generally very small, having only one or two rooms. Many of these houses had clay walls and thatched, gabled roofs in traditional west African styles. Some slave houses were raised above the ground, while others had dirt floors. The earliest slave homes that have been excavated had outdoor hearths for cooking—in west African custom, most daily activities (like cooking, sewing, and repairing tools) took place in the open—while later homes had indoor hearths in the middle of the floor, with stick and clay chimneys.

Shotgun Houses

The "shotgun house" is believed to have originated in central Africa and was brought to the American South by Haitians from the West Indies in the early part of the nineteenth century. It was given its odd name because of its long, linear layout—so that a shot fired through the front door or passage would pass straight through successive doorways to the end of the house. The typical shotgun house is one room wide and several rooms deep; most have front-facing gables or hipped roofs and modest front porches.

The Ubiquitous Front Porch

Few people know it, but the front porch was originally an African architectural feature that has become a standard for the American house. Typical of homes in hot, tropical climates, devised to provide shade and cross-ventilation for relief from the tropical heat and humidity, the porch was first introduced to the American South by slaves from west Africa. In addition to shade, the porch also serves as a communal gathering space—a function that is very important to African, Caribbean, and African American cultures.

ABOVE: *A modified double shotgun house in Atlanta, Georgia, built on brick piers, with a hipped roof and multiple porches.*

MARIE-THERESE METOYER'S HOUSE

The only known Congo-style structure in North America of the slavery era, the African House (c. 1800) at Melrose Plantation, Louisiana, was built under the direction of Marie-Therese Metoyer, a former slave who married into the owners' family. She designed the straw-thatched house after her home in Africa. The lower portion of the building is made of brick, and the upper portion, of large cypress timbers, with eaves that slope down, close to the ground.

WESTERN VERNACULAR

Following the California Gold Rush of 1849, a number of new towns sprang up in the so-called "Wild West." The migrants built their homes, stores, and barns in a practical, unpretentious vernacular style that often had little to do with the Victorian architecture that was prevalent elsewhere in the nation.

STYLE FILE

Notable Features:
Wood framing;
Gable or shed roofs;
Rectangular, plain
  wooden false-front
  facades, rising above
  the front-facing gable.

Major Influences:
Italianate style;
Gothic Revival;
Queen Anne style;
Stick style.

Where and When:
California and the North
  American West;
c. 1849–early 1900s.

False Fronts

The main streets of these new towns were lined with simple, wooden, gable- and shed-roofed commercial and residential structures of a number of disparate shapes and construction styles. Especially in the farming and mining communities of the Rocky Mountain states (including Nevada, Colorado, and Montana), it became popular to add a rectangular wooden facade that rose above the gable, to mimic the flat-roofed appearance of older, Italianate-style structures. This false front, so ubiquitous in Western movies, unified the look of these new town buildings and made them appear larger—and their owners more affluent—than they really were.

GHOST TOWNS

As the Gold Rush wound itself down to a trickle, many of the new Western mining towns simply died out—as did the false-front style. Though some Western main streets still sport false-fronted buildings, the style became an icon of the instability and transience of "boom" development. Today, all that remain of most ghost towns are disused, boarded-up structures in various states of decay.

Gold Fever

The promise of gold was the driving force behind many of the new towns that emerged, practically overnight, to dot the landscape of the Western frontier. However, by mid-1849, most of the "easy gold" had been extracted—and, though new prospectors continued to migrate westward in droves, relatively few found success. Further gold rushes included the 1897 Klondike strike, which attracted tens of thousands of people to the Yukon.

ABOVE: *A false-fronted building on the main street of a Western ghost town.*

OPPOSITE: *A period image of one of Nevada's first structures built by settlers.*

BELOW: *A weather-beaten barn on a vast Western ranch.*

Settling In

Some Western new towns survived the demise of the Gold Rush, stabilizing and maturing into more permanent communities, with the wooden false-front structures being gradually torn down and replaced by more substantial masonry buildings. At the same time, other (especially more affluent) vernacular homes of the Rocky Mountains show clear Victorian influences—in particular, Gothic Revival, Queen Anne, and Stick style —as well as Classical detailing.

SPANISH COLONIAL

The stereotypical Spanish Colonial building is recognizably Baroque in style: some of the finest Churrigueresque (*see* page 97) churches are found in Peru and Mexico. But not all Spanish Colonial buildings were this elaborate: sometimes local conditions, available skills, and materials demanded simpler styles.

Stylistic Evolution

Some of the finest Spanish Colonial architecture is found in Mexico. The Alhóndiga de Granaditas, or old granary, in Guanajuato, central Mexico, is among the best secular examples. Not surprisingly, though, the great religious buildings exemplify this style best. The Metropolitan Cathedral in Mexico City, begun in 1573, but not completed until 1813, has a frontage on the city square, or Zócalo, that represents the colonial Baroque at its best. To one side is the Churrigueresque (*see* page 97) facade of the adjoining Sagrario Metropolitano or parish church. Above, on either side, rise two bell towers of a later

OPPOSITE, ABOVE: *The Mission church of San Xavier del Bac, near Tucson, Arizona. The building shows influences ranging from Byzantine to Moorish and Baroque.*

RIGHT: *The decorative facade of Iglesia de San Francisco in Lima, Peru.*

vintage, designed by Manuel Tolsá at the end of the eighteenth century. Behind, above a traditional cross-shaped ground plan, is Tolsá's stunning dome.

While Mexico has the most surviving Spanish Colonial buildings, there are also splendid examples in Arizona, California, and New Mexico, and in the old towns of Santo Domingo, Dominican Republic; Cartagena, Colombia; Havana, Cuba; Santa Ana de Coro, Venezuela; and Lima, Peru.

"WHITE DOVE OF THE DESERT"

Dating from 1783, the mission church of San Xavier del Bac, Tucson, Arizona, was the work of several colonial architects, all unknown. The ravishing restraint of its exterior is lent emphasis by the dazzling whiteness of its stuccoed towers, and contrasts dramatically with the overwhelming richness of the frescoed walls and ceilings inside.

LEFT: *The church of Merced, Antigua Guatemala.*

LOG HOMES

Brought to the New World by German, Swedish, and other settlers of the middle colonies of Maryland, Pennsylvania, Delaware, and New Jersey—and later adopted across the North American continent—the log home has become a symbol of the independent, self-sufficient spirit of the American pioneers.

OPPOSITE: *The original section of this log house in Ohio dates from the seventeenth century; the shuttered foreground part was a later addition.*

BELOW: *A 1903 photograph showing a detail of a rustic log home in a pioneer community.*

The Log Cabin

Though some Northwestern peoples used wood planking in construction, the log home is modeled on imported, rather than adapted indigenous, techniques. The traditional log cabin was a simple, one-room dwelling with a single exterior chimney. It was constructed of round timbers that were joined at the corners by overlapping saddle notches. The open spaces between the logs were chinked with organic matter such as clay, moss, or mud. If more space was needed, an extra room could be added to the one-room cabin, with each

STYLE FILE

Notable Features:
Log Cabins: One- or two-room structures;
Round timbers joined by saddle notches;
Mud or moss chinking;
Single chimney outside the exterior wall (two-room structures with a central chimney or one at each end).
Continental Log Houses:
Three rooms;
Central chimney;
Round or square-hewn timbers;
Roofed front porch.

Major Influences:
European vernacular.

Where and When:
North America;
c. mid-1600s onward.

room having a separate exterior entranceway; while the chimney could become centrally located, at the roof ridgeline, or it could remain outside the wall of the gable end, with a second chimney added to the other end. Sometimes there was an upper loft area for sleeping. Some found it useful to add a roofed porch to the front of their log home.

Variations

As the log home spread southward and westward across the timber-rich regions of Appalachia and the Smoky Mountains, and through Canada, it was picked up by new waves of Scots–Irish and English immigrants, who adopted the Continental log-house plan—typically having three rooms and a central chimney. Another innovation was the two-room log house with a "dogtrot" (a center passageway). Some log houses had walls of square-hewn timbers, which made them sturdier and more weatherproof. Later log houses were often constructed with larger gaps between the timbers, which would then be weatherproofed with boards or shingles.

CARIBBEAN STYLES

Having been colonized by the British, Dutch, French, and Spanish, the architecture of the Caribbean reflects a variety of European influences. In addition to colonization, the Caribbean islands had a long history of slavery and waves of immigration, which brought African, Asian, Native American, and Indian building techniques and elements into the mix.

STYLE FILE

Notable Features:
Wood, stone, and coral;
Rectangular and low for
  hurricane resistance;
Gabled (often tin) roofs;
Large, open verandahs;
Sash and jalousie
  windows with shutters;
Terra-cotta tiles;
Elevation on stilts;
Pastel or vivid colors.

Major Influences:
European colonial,
  African, Asian, and
  North American styles.

Where and When:
Caribbean islands; late
  1600s–present.

Colonial Signatures

The British colonizers of the Caribbean built in a variety of British-inspired styles, including Georgian, Tudor, and Victorian. As an example, Barbados is dominated by British colonial architecture, which is more conservative, balanced, and uniform than that of some of the other islands, in contrast with the more flamboyant and ornamented structures built by the Spanish (who left behind a legacy of cathedrals and convents) and the French (with their ironwork market buildings). On Curaçao, which was settled by the Dutch, parts of the capital city, Willemstad, resemble Amsterdam or a provincial Dutch city, with gabled houses painted in pastel colors and with red roof tiles.

RIGHT: *Louvered shutter doors on a Curaçao house.*
BELOW: *A thatched* palapa *(or shade structure) in Honduras.*

ABOVE: *By elevating coastal houses on stilts, a certain amount of storm protection is provided, at least in terms of flooding; nowhere have building techniques been perfected against hurricane conditions.*

CONCH HOUSES

Energy-efficient in tropical heat, the classic conch houses of the Florida Keys draw on disparate influences. Originally handcrafted by seafaring carpenters, they combine Gulf Coast forms with styles from New England resorts and tropical Caribbean adaptations. A typical conch house has a gabled tin roof, a front porch, and a second-story verandah.

Climate Adaptations

In order to survive in the tropical Caribbean climate—which is windy, rainy, and hot—the European colonists built their houses with gable roofs and large, open verandahs, fitting windows with sturdy shutters. To make them earthquake- and hurricane-resistant, they built rectangular houses, low to the ground. Locally sourced materials included wood, stone (often limestone), and coral (which was the favored material for the "great houses" of the colonial sugar plantations, such as those found in Barbados). Many buildings across the islands are set upon stilts—a traditional Caribbean style of building that has existed since precolonial times, as a protection against storms and flooding. Excavations of a pre-Columbian stilt village unearthed off a 2-mile stretch of beach at Los Buchillones, on the north coast of Cuba, have yielded scattered house posts and postholes from homes built on dry land, as well as remnants of a thatched roof.

CLASSICISM REVIVED

The Renaissance had found inspiration in ancient Greek and Roman architecture, its order and symmetry suggesting what might be attainable by human reason, ingenuity, and enterprise. Those same values were at the fore in the Enlightenment of the eighteenth century, but by this time they were taking on a distinctly political edge. In its mounting revolutionary ferment, France was looking back to the heroic example of republican Rome—Jacques-Louis David's iconic painting *The Oath of the Horatii* was created in 1776. At this very moment across the Atlantic, the American colonies were engaged in their own fight for liberty; here too, freedom was to find expression in Classical forms.

OPPOSITE: *The Massachusetts State House (1798), in Boston, designed by Charles Bulfinch, with its magnificent gilded dome, is one of the finest Neoclassical buildings in the United States.*

PALLADIAN

No single architect did more to influence the rediscovery and reinvention of Classical architecture for the modern age than the Italian master Andrea Palladio. An important figure in his own lifetime, he was to loom still larger in later centuries as an influence, thus enjoying not one, but several, posthumous careers.

STYLE FILE

Notable Features:
Clear Classical influence, including column orders, with understated grace and symmetry;
Arched windows, and fanlights above doors;
Columns and pilasters.

Major Influences:
Italian Renaissance architect Palladio;
Greek and Roman buildings and features.

Where and When:
Britain, 17th–18th centuries; United States, 18th and 19th centuries.

BELOW: *The north facade of the White House.*

Majesty and Modesty

Key to Palladio's achievement (*see* page 83) was an understated simplicity that lent an unexpected air of intimacy to his grandest buildings. His basilica in Vicenza (c. 1547) and the Villa Rotonda that he built outside that city (c. 1567) are among the most celebrated examples of his work. Both rank among the most imposing of Renaissance monuments, yet their beauty sets us at our ease: we never seem to lose the human scale.

Of all the many hundreds of later Palladian creations around the world, perhaps the most typical example is Washington, D.C.'s, White House (1792–1800), which was designed by Irish architect James Hoban. The building bears similarities to Dublin's Leinster House and to other Irish Palladian mansions and civic structures. Its restraint is notable: there are no European palatial embellishments.

THE MASTER

Born Andrea di Pietro
della Gondola in Padua,
Italy,1508, this artist
was nicknamed Palladio
by a contemporary
critic. The name derives
from Pallas Athene, the
Greek goddess of
wisdom. A stonemason
by training, Palladio
made a close study of
Vitruvius and other
ancient theorists; his
work became the
conduit by which
Classical principles made
their way into the
architecture of the
modern age. Below, his
Villa Rotonda, Vicenza.

Anglo–Palladianism

The first great Palladian revival, however,
came as early as the seventeenth century,
when architects like Inigo Jones (1573–1652,
the creator of London's Covent Garden
Piazza) made it a part of the English scene.
Jones's Banqueting House (1619–22) at
Whitehall, London, was arguably the first
great example of this influential Anglo–
Palladian style. In the eighteenth century,
Palladianism enjoyed another revival, ush-
ered in by the Scottish architect Colin
Campbell (1676–1729) and Richard Boyle,
Lord Burlington (1694–1753). Designed with
the help of his friend, William Kent, the latter's masterpiece, London's Chiswick House
(1726), was explicitly modeled on Palladio's
original Villa Rotonda. Sir Christopher Wren
(1632–1723, *see also* pages 86–87) was
another adherent of the Palladian style.

ABOVE, LEFT: *The Radcliffe
Camera, a library at the
University of Oxford, designed
by James Gibbs, built 1737–49.*
BELOW: *A Palladian window
has an arch above, sometimes
with fanlight, and sidelights
enclosed by pilasters.*

FRENCH NEOCLASSICAL

The French Revolution of 1789 was the violent culmination of a wholesale intellectual overhaul that had occupied much of the eighteenth century. For artists and architects of the day, Rome represented not only republicanism, but an age apparently free of childish superstition and meddling clergy.

Unbuildable Ideals

French *philosophes* like Diderot and Voltaire were a thorn in the flesh of the Church and monarchy, but their rationalism found echoes even in establishment architecture. If the Classical influence is clear in constructions of this time, so, too, is a concern to capture the perfect, pure shapes of solid geometry. The cube, the sphere, the pyramid: these were the forms to which architects should aspire.

Obviously, no functional structure used by real people could possibly embody such perfection fully, but the closer the approximation, the better, the theorists thought. Architects like Etienne-Louis Boullée (1728–99) and Claude-Nicolas Ledoux (1736–1806) took these ideas so seriously that they designed idealized structures, never intended to take physical form. But Ange-Jacques Gabriel's (1698–1782) Petit Trianon, built in the

> **STYLE FILE**
>
> **Notable Features:**
> Basic vocabulary (orders of columns, arches, etc.) Classical, but an interest in attaining a three-dimensional symmetry and "natural" simplicity.
>
> **Major Influences:**
> Enlightenment rationalism a reaction against all relics of monarchism and clericalism; Rousseauesque ideas of "natural" proportions.
>
> **Where and When:**
> France; 18th century.

BELOW: *The Petit Trianon, Versailles (1761–64).*

grounds of the royal palace at Versailles, near Paris (1761–64), shows the beautiful realities such architecture could achieve.

The Perfect Panthéon

The Panthéon, in Paris, was built between 1757 and 1790 to a design by Jacques-Germain Soufflot. Its most obvious models may be the ancient Pantheon and St. Peter's Cathedral, both in Rome, but it also bears the imprint of the theories of its time. If its austere, unfussy symmetries suggest the rationalism of Boullée and Ledoux, its overwhelming simplicity evokes the values of Laugier (*see* feature). That said, the Panthéon is actually a good deal less simple than it looks: it is, in fact, an example of two-in-one construction. Outside, massive walls bear up the bulk of the building's weight—including, with the help of hidden flying buttresses, the shapely dome. The spacious interior aisles can thus be supported with only slender columns.

ABOVE AND BELOW: *The Panthéon, Paris, was modeled on the Pantheon of ancient Rome* (see *page 25*).

GERMAN NEOCLASSICAL

Berlin was the showcase of what is known as German Neoclassicism, though Prussian Neoclassicism might be a more apt label, as the city was the capital of the state of Prussia during its heyday in the eighteenth and nineteenth centuries.

Grand and Grander

The first Neoclassical building in Germany was the Schloss Bellevue (1786), an elegant, formal structure with Corinthian columns framing its central entrance. Designed by Philipp Daniel Boumann, it was built as a summer residence for the Prussian royal family. (Today it remains an important landmark as an official residence for Germany's president.)

But the most iconic structure of this style is the monumental Brandenburg Gate, commissioned by Friedrich Wilhelm II of Prussia in 1789 as one of a series of gates into Berlin, and clearly designed to make a statement. With its twelve Doric columns, it was modeled on the Propylaea (gateway) at the Acropolis in Athens. The goddess of victory in a quadriga, or four-horse chariot, surmounts the huge gateway. Its architect, Karl Gotthard Langhans, was a lawyer, mathematician, and enthusiastic Classicist whose other significant architectural achievements included the National Theatre (1800–2) in Berlin.

STYLE FILE

Notable Features:
Ancient Greek temples;
Monumental structures
  designed to impress;
Symmetry, decorative
  restraint. formal lines.

Major Influences:
European Neoclassicism,
  especially Palladian amd
  Georgian styles.

Where and When:
Germany, especially
  Berlin; late 18th and
  early 19th century.

BELOW: *The Bellevue Palace, or Schloss, in Berlin is considered the first major building of German Neoclassicism.*

Rebuilding Berlin

The march of Napoleon's forces into Berlin in 1806 halted the city's growth, but the French occupation would last less than a decade. An ambitious remodeling programme followed, headed by Karl Friedrich Schinkel, who designed a series of Neoclassical monuments, including the Neue Wache (a military guard post, 1816–18); an imposing theatre (1819–21) on the Gendarmenmarkt, to replace Langhans' edifice after it burned down; and the Altes Museum (Old Museum, 1823–30) on Museum Island. In all these buildings, the influence of the ancient Greeks is explicit.

ABOVE: *The Reichstag, Berlin, in 1900, six years after its completion. Its design emulated the Neoclassical buildings of the earlier half of the century.*
TOP: *Schinkel's theatre and concert hall on the Gendarmenmarkt, Berlin.*
RIGHT: *Brandenburg Gate, detail, once again a symbolic portal after reunification.*

GEORGIAN

England has had no fewer than six King Georges, but in architectural terms the word "Georgian" refers to the reigns of the monarchs George I–IV (1714–1837). The style had its heyday between about 1730 and 1800, a period seen as something of a golden age in British architectural history.

Quiet Good Taste

This was the age of the "Grand Tour," when any young gentleman with pretensions to taste and education made a point of spending several months traveling the continent of Europe. The ruins of Greece and Rome were particular attractions, and the clear inspiration for the sort of architecture that was coming into fashion at home.

Balance and unshowy, tasteful elegance were the most important characteristics of this Georgian style, just as they were deemed the most precious attributes of the refined Georgian gentleman. This was a paradoxical architecture, assertively unassuming; a style that dared to do away with ostentation: gone were the scrolls and curlicues and other ornamentation of the Baroque.

STYLE FILE

Notable Features:
Neoclassical principles;
Strict symmetry;
Tall townhouses, often in regimented terraces;
Multipaned windows, sometimes curved tops;
Corniced, often dentilled.

Major Influences:
Classical architecture;
Mass production of brick and sheet glass;
Increasing wealth of landowning aristocracy and middle class.

Where and When:
Britain, Ireland, eastern United States;
c. 1730–1840.

A Decorous Display

Unobtrusiveness was the watchword: simple sash windows with thin pane glass were used to punctuate plain walls of brick or painted plaster. Smaller windows at lower-story level allowed for greater solidity, but bigger windows let light stream into second-story reception rooms, the center of the house. Houses had three, or even four, stories: in the cities particularly they were built high, allowing a sense of roominess and ease in the minimum of footprint space. Paneled-wood front doors, frequently topped with semicircular window vents with radiating fanlights, completed the effect of gracious functionality.

What else is there to be said? The accent was on unassertiveness. If Georgian architects went for spectacular effects, it was not in the individual building, but in the mass. Splendid terraces of townhouses were laid out in sweeping "circuses" and crescents, most famously, perhaps, in the cities of Bath, England, and Edinburgh, Scotland. Similar developments were built in the higher-toned neighborhoods of America's eastern cities.

ABOVE: *Classical Georgian terraces in London (left) and Bath, Somerset (right).*
OPPOSITE: *Trinity College, Dublin, Ireland.*

DUBLIN'S FAIR CITY

For a time after 1782, the Irish parliament had unprecedented autonomy: Ireland remained British, but Dublin was a quasicapital. The building boom that followed showed how much more there was to Georgian design than the townhouse (though there were plenty of those). A fine custom house, parliament house, law courts, and other public buildings were all constructed, as well as several of the most handsome churches anywhere in the British Isles.

145

FEDERALIST/ADAM

So-called because it dates from the first decades of the United States' existence, "Federal" architecture was influenced by British models. The Scottish brothers Robert (1728–92) and James Adam (1732–94) were a major influence.

STYLE FILE

Notable Features:
Simple, Classical lines
  and proportions, but
  comparatively elaborate
  decoration, both inside
  and out;
Low-pitched roofs
  screened by stone
  balustrades;
Shuttered windows.

Major Influences:
Classical principles,
  especially Palladian;
Georgian houses;
Republican ideals.

Where and When:
Britain, 18th century;
  Federal style, United
  States, 1776–c.1800.

ABOVE: *Bute House, Charlotte Square, Edinburgh, is today the official residence of Scotland's First Minister. Designed by Robert Adam, it features a Palladian doorway and central window, with ornamentation typical of Adams' style.*

Antiquarian Adam

Robert in particular had made an enthusiastic study of ancient monuments, including the newly excavated ruins of Pompeii, Italy. His ancient inspirations, however, were not just Roman, but Etruscan, and even Egyptian— and he noted interior design and decoration as well as external forms. Where his countrymen were content to evoke the symmetrical spirit of Classical architecture, he worked Roman motifs directly into his work. Commissioned to design the south front of Kedleston Hall, a country house in the English Midlands, for example, he used as its centerpiece a four-story reproduction of the magnificent Arch of Constantine in Rome (*see* page 22).

Fun Without Frivolity

Just as distinctively Adamesque, however, were the little decorative touches he used to counterpoint the severities of Neoclassical design. Flat panels and pilasters broke up blank walls; decorative devices, from urns and arabesques to stucco scrolls and sphinxes, adorned interiors: the final effect combined vigor and visual interest with sobriety.

The New Republic

As such it was the ideal style for the newly independent United States—proud and self-confident, yet still recognizably puritanical in its values. That the Adam style bore more resemblance to Roman models than English only enhanced it in American eyes. Not that U.S. architects were content simply to replicate the Adam style: over time, they would make it very much their own. Their innovations ranged from the flagrantly patriotic (the use of the eagle motif) through the practical (the addition of decorative window shutters) to the more subtle (the introduction of oval and elliptical shapes for windows and even rooms).

> **SWAGS**
>
> Carved swags of stone, stucco, or wood were a feature of Federalist buildings: these decorative bouquets and festoons adorned everything from ceilings and paneled walls to furniture. Generally comprising flowers, fruit, sheafs of grain, or other produce, they lent an air of elegant Classicism and comfort at the same time. Harking back to the decorative art of ancient Rome, as symbols of fertility and plenty they also struck a real chord with what was still an agricultural society.

BELOW: *Adelphi Terrace (left), London (1768–74, demolished 1936), built by the brothers Adam. Faneuil Hall (right), Boston (built 1740–42, but with significant later alterations).*

JEFFERSONIAN

Quite how closely "Federalist" architecture was bound up with the constitutional construction of the United States becomes clear when the role of founding father Thomas Jefferson is considered. The third president is famous for his range of interests, of course, and architecture was one passion among many, but it would be quite wrong to dismiss his talent as a mere hobby.

STYLE FILE

Notable Features:
Self-consciously
Neoclassical architec-
ture, often closely
modeled on actual
Roman examples.

Major Influences:
Work of Adam brothers
in Britain;
Existing Federalist work
in the United States.

Where and When:
The United States;
c. 1770–1830.

Architectural *Amour*

"Here I am, Madame, gazing whole hours at the Maison Quarrée, like a lover at his mistress…" So the then-minister to France wrote in a letter to his friend the Comtesse de Tessé. The object of his ardor was a Roman temple near Nîmes, the sheer simplicity of whose design does indeed take the breath away. Built to a straightforward rectangular ground plan (its French nickname means, literally, "square house"), its appeal lies in its perfect proportions and quiet grace, and the effect of weightlessness suggested by its shapely columns.

LEFT: *Monticello, Jefferson's Virginia home, which served as an "architectural laboratory."*

A Technical Revolution

The one adaptation Jefferson made when he took this temple as the model for his Virginia State Capitol in Richmond (1785–89) was to substitute simpler Ionic capitals for the Corinthian originals. This was a concession to what he feared would be the technical inferiority of American stonemasons. Thanks to Jefferson, in fact, in the years that followed they would become accomplished in the whole repertoire of Classical sculpting skills.

"An Academical Village"

Jefferson's last great architectural project was for the new University of Virginia at Charlottesville (1817–26). Though the circular library is clearly based on the Pantheon in Rome, the overall impression is of a sort of stylized Athens. Living accommodation is concealed in templelike pavilions, facing each other across an open area recalling the ancient Agora and linked by colonnaded walkways like the Athenian *stoi*. Beautiful as the buildings are, the overall conception was arguably finer still: Jefferson's vision of the university as civic community lives on in the campus colleges of modern times.

OPPOSITE: *An aerial view of the graceful Virginia State Capitol, Richmond.*

THE LABORATORY

Jefferson's home, at Monticello, Virginia, has been described as an "architectural laboratory." The future president began building in 1770, his original inspiration Palladian, but making all sorts of idiosyncratic innovations of his own. Making full use of the natural contours, he concealed the more functional rooms in L-shaped wings or "dependencies" stretching away behind the main building. He placed the main windows so as to make the two-story structure appear to have only one. The overall effect is to give a big house the beautiful simplicity of a cottage, to give grandeur a "democratic" air.

GREEK REVIVAL

It wasn't just Jefferson's designs, but his commissions that made a difference to the development of American architecture. Increasingly, these, too, tended toward the Greek Revival style, with its columns and pediments.

A Transatlantic Athens

In 1803, as president, Jefferson appointed Benjamin Henry Latrobe (1766–1820) to supervise construction of the U.S. Capitol (*see* page 15). In his Bank of Pennsylvania, Philadelphia (1799), built very much along the lines of an Athenian temple, Latrobe had already shown his enthusiasm for the "pure" architectural forms of ancient Greece. His own work in this style found its ultimate expression in the Roman Catholic Basilica, Baltimore (1806–21, *see also* page 159), but it was developed in works by William Strickland (1788–1854) like the Second Bank of the U.S. in Philadelphia (1819–24). In the Old World as in America, the Greek Revival was gathering momentum: by mid-century, it seemed, the style held sway. Enriched by the

Industrial Revolution, Britain's provincial cities had a degree of civic pride and pretension that prompted them to identify with the achievements of ancient Greece and Rome. The outstanding example is, perhaps, that of Glasgow, Scotland, then grown to prominence as the second city of the British Empire, whose leading citizens set out to construct an appropriately grandiose architectural heritage almost from scratch. It seemed almost inevitable that the preferred medium for this should be the Classical style favored by leading local architects like Alexander "Greek" Thomson (1817–75).

Back to the Future

Neoclassicism had become the "natural" medium for any expression of pride in architecture. When, in the 1870s, a newly unified Germany first envisaged a national parliament building in Berlin, it was no surprise that a design in this style was chosen. Paul Wallot (1841–1912) was its architect. When it was constructed in 1884–94, the *Reichstag's* glass-and-steel cupola represented an engineering breakthrough, but its aesthetic principles had been laid down over 2,000 years before.

> **GONE WITH THE WIND?**
>
> When Hurricane Katrina (2005) tore through Louisiana, she caused physical devastation—but also did untold damage to the regional economy. Left physically intact, but hit hard by the subsequent collapse of the tourist industry, was one of the South's most perfect jewels of architecture, Oak Alley Plantation, near Vacherie. The oak avenue after which the plantation was named was planted in the early eighteenth century, but the Greek Revival-style house (1837–39) is arguably an even more stunning sight.

TOP: *Oak Alley Plantation.*

OPPOSITE, RIGHT: *Latrobe's Baltimore Basilica.*

OPPOSITE, LEFT: *A church in Glasgow, Scotland, designed by Alexander "Greek" Thomson.*

ENGLISH REGENCY

Between 1811 and 1820, King George III being afflicted by mental illness, Britain was ruled on his behalf by a regent: his son, the future King George IV. It was an unhappy time for the country, but one of achievement in architecture.

Definitions

The word "regency" is often used loosely, and can refer to architecture dating from any time between 1800 and 1830; some see it as no more than a subsection of the Georgian age. These are mere matters of categorization, of course; more important is the fact that the aesthetic continuities are clear. The sheer energy and creativity of Regency architecture entitles it to separate consideration, but it shares the general Georgian preoccupation with poise and understated elegance.

Terraced Splendor

The Regency townhouse was typically an impressive edifice. Often bow-fronted, it had higher, more eye-catching windows than its Georgian predecessors. Usually built of

"HINDOO GOTHIC"

Despised for his decadence, "Georgie Porgie" (the English prince regent, later King George IV) was held in as much contempt as his father, "Farmer George" (George III), was in affection. It seemed only appropriate, then, that his greatest legacy should have been something of an architectural folly— the Exotic (see pages 176–77) Royal Pavilion at the southern English seaside resort of Brighton, built 1815–23. Designed by John Nash (1752–1835), the premier architect of the Regency style, it juxtaposes Classical columns with mock-Mughal minarets and domes—a token of English imperial interest in India. At first much ridiculed, this palatial extravaganza has since earned admiration for its originality and vision.

brick, it gleamed with white stucco or painted plaster, and was entered up imposing steps through pilastered porches. For all that, it may be seen from a modern point of view as lacking "character." This, however, is to miss the point: the Regency was an age of fashion. Emulation was arguably more important than individual expression: "keeping up with the Joneses" was everything. If the Englishman's home was still his castle, he was happy for it to be subsumed aesthetically into a larger architectural vision of which it was just a uniform component part. Hence the importance, even more than for the earlier Georgians, of the great sweeping terrace of townhouses, of the type to be seen in such genteel resorts as Cheltenham and Brighton, as well, of course, as London. Altogether, these terraces could be truly awesome in scale—often they had triumphal arches at their entrances—though each householder only had a bit-part in the greater glory.

VICTORIAN STYLES

If the early years of the nineteenth century were, on the whole, dominated in architectural terms by the Classical Revival styles, this was all about to change. Not only was technology moving on apace, but international trade and cultural awareness of the wider world were increasing steadily. The choice of building materials was growing, industry was burgeoning, new towns and cities were emerging, and structures large and small could be fashioned in diverse styles that borrowed elements from many traditions. Architects continued to look to the past for inspiration—particularly to the Gothic age—but they also created entirely new ways to build, liberated by technical and material advances from the structural constraints that had determined the limits of their predecessors' choices.

OPPOSITE: *The entrance to the opulent Biltmore Estate (built 1888–95), a 250-room Chateauesque-style home near Asheville, North Carolina, designed by Richard Morris Hunt for George W. Vanderbilt. Now a National Historic Landmark, it was once the largest private home in the United States; its extensive gardens were landscaped by Frederick Law Olmsted, creator of Manhattan's Central Park.*

GOTHIC REVIVAL

Some historians consider the term "Gothic Revival" a misnomer because Gothic architecture persisted in Europe from medieval times through succeeding centuries without entirely fading from use. But the widespread readoption of Gothic decoration emerged in England, France, and Germany in the early nineteenth century; by mid-century, it had swept across North America.

STYLE FILE

Notable Features:
Pointed arches over
  doors and windows;
Interior vaulting;
Steeply pitched roofs;
Tall turrets;
Pinnacles and finials;
Crenelations;
Angular chimneys;
Leaded glass.

Major Influences:
Gothic architecture.

Where and When:
Western Europe and
  North America; 19th
  century.

The Rise of Romanticism

In England, prominent architects—even some Neoclassicists—continued to apply Gothic features to ecclesiastical buildings well before the rise of the Romantic movement that inspired the Gothic Revival. One notable example is Sir Christopher Wren's 1681 "Tom Tower" at the chapel of Christ Church, University of Oxford. But the first celebration of Gothic decoration per se is attributed to Horace Walpole, who refashioned his country estate near London with fanciful decorative features—exterior and interior—including turrets, pointed arches, and crockets. This eighteenth-century confection gave rise to the label "Strawberry Hill Gothic," named for his famous estate.

RIGHT: *The Bridge of Sighs at St. John's College, Cambridge, an English Gothic Revival landmark designed by Henry Hutchinson and built in 1831.*

OPPOSITE: *The Peace Tower (1927) on Parliament Hill, Ottawa. Canada's parliament buildings (1857–66; subsequent remodeling after fire damage) were all designed in the Gothic Revival style.*

Crossing the Atlantic

The first American Gothic Revival building, Glen Ellen in Baltimore, was designed in 1832 by Alexander Jackson Davis, who would become the nation's most prolific Gothic Revival architect. In 1837 he published a book of house plans that introduced the style to the masses. Its popularity was further advanced by two pattern books by Davis's colleague Andrew Jackson Downing, who offered the middle classes more affordable alternatives to the expensive stone Gothic–style mansions.

Meanwhile, the Gothic Revival also gained exposure in the United States through the high-profile projects of architects like Richard Upjohn, an Englishman whose landmarks included New York City's Trinity Church (1846). Soon, the Gothic style was everywhere: picturesque cottages flourished in the countryside with multiple gables, turrets, and wide porches, and elements of the style were adapted for use in city houses—like the Gothic door, window, and cornice detailing.

ABOVE: *The Scots Baronial Glengorm Castle (1860), near Tobermory, on the Isle of Mull, off Scotland's west coast. Like many similar mansions, this has been converted into a hotel.*

HIGH VICTORIAN GOTHIC

The Gothic Revival had begun with a romantic fascination for medieval ornamentation. But Anglo–French architect and craftsman A.W.N. Pugin introduced a moral dimension into the debate, rejecting the superficial use of medieval forms and advocating a return to "authentic" Gothic construction.

RIGHT: *Facade detail of George Gilbert Scott's St. Pancras Station, London (1874).*
BELOW: *Return of the gargoyle.*

Function and Craftsmanship

Pugin made the case for returning to the structural integrity of medieval buildings—the use of buttresses, ribs, and so on—rather than simply overlaying Gothic elements on more modern structures. He also extolled the superior craftsmanship of the medieval artisan and exhorted his contemporaries to emulate them rather than accepting shoddy or machine-made goods. Pugin's finest hour was his contribution to the richly ornamented interiors at the U.K. Houses of Parliament in London's Westminster (built 1840–60).

Pugin's beliefs influenced the work of architectural theorist John Ruskin, a founder of the Arts and Crafts movement (*see* pages 192–93). Ruskin's advocacy of craftsmanship, beauty, and historical authenticity helped lay the foundations of a new generation of ecclesiastical and public buildings, even if not all were constructed with the medieval materials and methods that he so admired.

RIGHT: *The elaborately ornamented Houses of Parliament (built 1840–60), Westminster, London, designed by Charles Barry, with A.W.N. Pugin.*

NORTH AMERICAN GOTHIC CHURCHES

The illustrious architect Benjamin H. Latrobe submitted both Classical and Gothic designs for the first Catholic cathedral in the United States, the Basilica of the Assumption (1806–21, see page 150), Baltimore. The Classical plan was chosen, but his Gothic design was an inspiration to other architects, who would go on to design a plethora of churches in the Gothic Revival style, which would emerge as the principal form of ecclesiastical architecture in the United States and Canada by the middle of the nineteenth century.

From Masonry to "Iron Gothic"

In Britain and North America, the High Victorian Gothic was characterized by ornate facades and multiple arches, turrets, multipaned windows, gables, and other vertically styled elements. They might have patterned facades of polychromatic masonry, like George Gilbert Scott's St. Pancras Station, London (1874), or intricate carvings and minutely detailed windows, like London's Houses of Parliament. In France, meanwhile, architect Eugène Viollet-le-Duc (1814–79) made his name with ambitious restorations of the great landmarks of French Gothic architecture. Rather than adhering to medieval materials, however, he advocated the use of modern alternatives, notably cast iron. His influence on Victorian architects—and, indeed, on such early modern-era designers as Antonio Gaudí—was profound.

ROMANESQUE REVIVAL

The origins of this popular Victorian architectural style lie in Germany, where the *Rundbogenstil*, or "round-arch style," took off in the early nineteenth century, and in Classical and medieval construction and decoration.

STYLE FILE

Notable Features:
Rounded arches;
Asymmetrical ground
  plans and facades;
Heavy stone walls;
Decorative belt courses;
Polychromatic masonry;
Medieval ornamentation,
  e.g., quatrefoil or
  roseate windows and
  decorative carvings;
Decorative, arched,
  recessed entryways.

Major Influences:
Romanesque;
Medieval styles.

Where and When:
North America, Europe;
  mid-to-late 1800s.

RIGHT: The recessed-arch entry to the south tower at the Smithsonian Institution's "Castle" building, which has many Romanesque features.

OPPOSITE, ABOVE: The Rundbogenstil cathedral at Speyer, Germany, designed by Heinrich Hübsch in the 1850s.

OPPOSITE, BELOW: The North-Evans Chateau (1870s) in Austin, Texas. Its use of rusticated stone prefigures Richardson (see pages 174–75).

The Economics of Fashion

With features such as grand, rounded arches, domes, and conical-topped towers, masonry buildings and mansions in the Romanesque Revival style were not cheap to build. But, in the late nineteenth century, America, where the style flourished, was enjoying a rush of wealth and technology that lent itself to the building of lavishly imposing public buildings designed in a variety of revival styles. The commanding Romanesque style naturally lent itself to the construction of major public buildings. However, some private homes were also constructed in this style; those that remain today (which look much like small, medieval stone castles) can be found mostly in cities that were wealthy in the Victorian era in the northeastern United States.

THE SMITHSONIAN INSTITUTION "CASTLE"

Location: Washington, D.C.
Date: 1847–55.
Architect: James Renwick.
Materials: Red sandstone from Maryland.
Significance: One of the most significant buildings of the pre–Civil War Romanesque Revival, the Smithsonian Institution's first building (now popularly known as "the Castle") was largely responsible for introducing this style to Americans, and it was viewed as the herald of a new era of American architecture. At the time, medieval-influenced styles were considered the most appropriate for educational buildings.

European and Classical Roots

The German *Rundbogenstil* arose as a reaction against Gothic Revival architecture. The aim was to evoke the grandeur of buildings in the Neoclassical styles. With prominent rounded arches like those of Roman buildings, the new style was functional and less ornate than contemporary revivals.

RENAISSANCE REVIVAL

Opulent turn-of-the-century Renaissance Revival buildings mimic the styles of the Italian and French Renaissance; they are both elegant and explicitly formal. Because the elaborate style required highly skilled craftsmanship and expensive materials, such as ashlar, it is mainly seen in large-scale public and commercial buildings and luxurious mansions for the wealthy.

STYLE FILE

Notable Features:
Symmetrical facades;
Smooth ashlar walls;
Quoins;
Blind arcading;
Architrave-framed,
  ornate windows;
Centrally located doors,
  framed by pilasters,
  supporting entablatures
  or pediments;
Horizontal stone banding
  dividing the ground story
  from the upper stories;
Smaller square windows
  on the top story;
Low-pitched hipped or
  mansard roofs;
Roofline entablatures,
  topped with balustrade.

Major Influences:
European Renaissance;
Classical buildings.

Where and When:
Europe, North America;
c. 1840–1920.

Rebirth of the Classical

The word "Renaissance" means "rebirth," and refers to the period in Europe in the fifteenth and sixteenth centuries in which literature, art, and architecture flourished, beginning in Italy. During this time, an educated cultural elite, and the artists and craftsmen that it sponsored, studied and admired the intellectual and artistic accomplishments of Classical antiquity. Renaissance Revival architecture also looks back to Classical antiquity, but unlike its Renaissance predecessors, it is often seen as derivative and lacking subtlety, with many eclectic and lavish features combined in a single building. Renaissance Revival buildings were, critics say, built for the wealthy to impress rather than embodying an artistic vision. In the United States, the style is most often seen in ostentatious mansions, while in Europe, the style was especially popular for public buildings in newly prosperous cities of the confident, industrial Victorian age.

RIGHT: *Neuschwanstein Castle, built 1869–86 for Ludwig I of Bavaria, Germany, reviving Renaissance features and scale.*

OPPOSITE: *The Breakers, designed by Richard Morris Hunt, Newport, Rhode Island.*

A Second Revival

Some of the Renaissance Revival architects were graduates of the *École des Beaux-Arts* in Paris, though their buildings perhaps lacked the restraint more often associated with the school. Opulent homes were popularly built in North America during "boom" periods, and especially in the "gilded age" of the late nineteenth century. The architect most associated with this period is the exuberant Richard Morris Hunt, who conceived many of the mansions of fashionable Newport, Rhode Island. Later Renaissance Revival homes are often larger and more elaborate, and are characterized by: columns supporting entablatures, arched, recessed openings, and balconies; full entablatures between story levels; and a ground-story facade of rusticated stone. Usually, each story of these homes is expressed differently (so that if the Doric order is used on the first story, then the next story will be of the Ionic or Corinthian orders, and so on). Many of these features can be seen at the Breakers, featured here.

ITALIANATE

Inspired by the architecture of rural Italy, the Italianate style (also known as Bracketed, Tuscan, or Lombard style) was adopted by English architects in the late 1830s as a romantic rebellion against the Classical styles that had prevailed in architectural design for the previous two centuries, and soon swept America.

STYLE FILE

Notable Features:
Square, rectangular, or
  L-shaped massing with
  a vertical emphasis;
Square cupolas or towers;
Elaborate detailing;
Overhanging eaves with
  decorative brackets;
Tall, narrow windows,
  usually arched or curved
  at the top;
Side bay windows;
Windows along the
  facade aligned in threes
  above the doorway;
Low-pitched or flat roofs;
Centered front-facing
  gables, or cross-hipped
  or crossed-gabled
  (L-shaped plans);
Wood framing;
Arcaded porches with
  balustraded balconies.

Major Influences:
Rural Italian buildings;
Renaissance styles.

Where and When:
Western Europe and
  the United States;
  c. 1840–85.

A Plastic Style

The Italianate style was made fashionable in America in part by the designs of Calvert Vaux and Alexander Jackson Davis, which were published in the pattern books of Andrew Jackson Downing. The style was widely adopted because of its highly adaptable nature: it could be as romantic as the Gothic or as reserved as the Neoclassical, making it suitable for a range of tastes and budgets. These houses are common everywhere except the Deep South (which was wracked with the economic hardship of the Civil War during the period in which the popularity of the style was at its height). The decline of the Italianate style in the United States is associated with the financial panic of 1873.

ABOVE: *This Italianate villa is typical of the style at its height in the United States. Its square massing, vertical emphasis, low-pitched roof, and bracketed eaves are some of its notable features.*

Cast-iron Palaces

The development of the cast-iron and pressed-metal industries in the mid-nineteenth century allowed for the cost-effective large-scale production of many of the Italianate decorative elements. These included cornices and brackets, which were previously made of carved stone. A number of U.S. cities have historic

neighborhoods featuring cast-iron-clad buildings that resemble grand Italian villas. In addition to new mansions and commercial buildings, colonial-style homes were often extensively remodeled during the late nineteenth century to incorporate these highly fashionable Italianate features.

ABOVE: *Cliveden, an English mansion built in 1851 in the Italianate style.*

BELOW: *A handsome townhouse in Detroit, Michigan, displaying the decorative elements typical of an Italianate villa.*

ITALIANATE DETAILING

Italianate detailing is most distinctive in windows, doorways, and eaves. Windows are often in pairs, curved or arched at the top, with single- or double-pane glazing. Sometimes the entire window is framed with elaborate detailing. Italianate window crowns may be hooded, bracketed, and/or pedimented. Doorways are heavily ornamented in a similar fashion, with double doors being common. Most houses in this style have either small front porches or full-width porches supported by square posts with beveled corners. Along the cornice line, large eave brackets in a variety of shapes are set singly or in twos.

CARPENTER GOTHIC

This style flourished in mid-nineteenth century America and was an evolution of the Gothic Revival in residential architecture, made possible by the advent of the steam-powered scroll saws that were used to create the elaborate ornamental woodwork. It was popularized by A.J. Downing's pattern books.

STYLE FILE

Notable Features:
Pointed, steep, intersecting Gothic gables;
Pointed-arched windows;
Cupolas and towers;
Asymmetrical floor plan;
Large verandahs;
Opulent appliqué work, scrollwork, pinnacles, finials, bargeboards, moldings, balustrades, and stickwork;
Intricate paintwork.

Major Influences:
Gothic Revival;
Queen Anne;
Stick style.

Where and When:
United States; c. 1840–90 (Canada: see text).

Angles and Planes

The Gothic Revival movement began with stone structures, but as new machinery made wood framing and wooden ornamentation widely and inexpensively available in the United States, Gothic styling was applied to ordinary domestic buildings. The lighter balloon-framed walls allowed for more complex building shapes, and precut ornamental features could be purchased by mail order. The overall appearance of the Carpenter Gothic house is of angular asymmetry and verticality, with pointed gables and windows, towers, steeply pitched roofs, and carved wooden ornaments, especially on gables and porches. In addition to the carved and appliquéd tracery and detailing, careful paintwork was sometimes used to enhance the decorative effect (*see* Steamboat Gothic, pages 184–85).

RIGHT: *Carpenter Gothic detailing on this California Victorian is enhanced by its carefully applied paintwork. Its tower, bays and window detail are typical of Queen Anne houses (see pages 170–71).*

LEFT: *The steep gables, ornate woodwork, and asymmetry of this well-preserved home identify it as Carpenter Gothic.*

INSET, BELOW: *The Carson House, Eureka, California, an experiment in opulence that has the qualities of a fairy-tale castle.*

Many cottages built in this style featured steep cross-gables or, on smaller examples, gabled porches. Bay and oriel windows were commonly seen, almost invariably sporting pointed arches and elaborate ornamentation and paintwork. On homes influenced by the Stick style, board-and-batten trim was used.

New England and Beyond
The Carpenter Gothic craze was taken up most enthusiastically in rural settings in the Northeast, and particularly in the summer residences of the wealthy, fashionable elite of the period. Martha's Vineyard, Massachusetts, Round Lake, New York, and Cape May, New Jersey, boast many examples; others can be seen in the Midwest and California. In Canada, the term "Carpenter Gothic" refers to a Gothic Revival structure built of wood, whether or not elaborately ornamented.

THE CARSON HOUSE

Location: Eureka, California.
Date: 1884–86.
Architect: Samuel Newsom.
Materials: Various types of wood.
Significance: This ornate mansion is said to be the most photographed Victorian house in the United States.

STICK STYLE

This indigenous American residential architectural style is characterized by patterned wood-plank cladding on the exterior walls—a practice that had been adapted from medieval European building styles.

STYLE FILE

Notable Features:
Patterned (horizontal, vertical, or diagonal) wooden plank or shingle cladding;
Gabled roofs and dormers;
Decorative trusses and support braces;
Wide, overhanging eaves with exposed rafter ends or brackets;
Porches;
Bay windows.

Major Influences:
Medieval English;
Gothic Revival;
Carpenter Gothic;
Alpine styles.

Where and When:
The United States;
c. 1860–80.

A Fleeting Fancy

The exterior woodwork that characterized this style appeared to mirror the structural beams of the building, giving a superficial resemblance to medieval half-timbering. The fact that the Stick style can appear angular, even austere, meant that it was easily overshadowed by the more ornate Victorian styles that nineteenth-century Americans found so appealing. The style thus enjoyed a relatively brief span of popularity, in the 1860s and '70s. Today, only a few intact examples remain.

Subtle Details

Unlike those of many of the more ostentatious Victorian styles, Stick-style builders favored flat, one-dimensional detailing in the form of horizontal, vertical, or diagonal patterns and lines along the exterior walls, which became known as "stickwork." The relatively

RIGHT: *Stickwork on a well-preserved Victorian home. This house also displays features typical of the Shingle Style (see pages 172–73).*

subtle ornamentation was often lost when these homes were remodeled, or simply covered with siding, which helps to explain why there are relatively few examples of Stick-style homes left to see.

ABOVE: *The Griswold House, Newport, Rhode Island, designed by R.M. Hunt (1862).*

Where to See the Stick Style

Today, restored Stick-style homes can be found in concentrated numbers in parts of San Francisco, where copious supplies of timber and a flourishing economy encouraged wooden-home construction during the 1870s and 1880s. Sometimes referred to as "painted ladies," these row-house versions of the Stick style usually have flat (rather than pitched) roofs. Other Stick-style homes can be found in coastal New England, with a number of fine examples in Hartford, Connecticut. In addition, there are many vernacular U.S. buildings that display elements of the style.

RESORT HOMES

The Stick style flourished during the heyday of the American summer beach resort. In places like Newport, Rhode Island, and Cape May, New Jersey, the style was popular for seaside cottages designed to be inhabited during the warm summer months. Stick-style beach homes frequently featured porches (providing a place to escape from the heat) and bay windows (for a better view of the ocean).

QUEEN ANNE

Of all the Victorian housing styles popular in North America, the eclectic Queen Anne was the most widespread, and some consider it to be the quintessential Victorian style—the culmination of everything that had come before it.

STYLE FILE

Notable Features:
Irregularly shaped,
  steeply pitched roofs;
Front-facing gables;
Decorative chimneys and
  gable ornaments;
Large porches extending
  along exterior walls;
Bay and oriel windows;
Circular corner towers;
Overhangs and wall
  projections;
Spacious floor plans;
Patterned shingles and/or
  stonework panels;
Stained glass or small,
  decorative panes.

Major Influences:
Gothic Revival;
English Tudor styles;
Charles Locke Eastlake.

Where and When:
Principally North America;
c. 1850–1900.

Above: *An 1890s, suburban Queen Anne house in Washington State.*

Opposite: *Probably the most famous row of Queen Anne townhouses anywhere, these "painted ladies" are among the most photographed buildings in San Francisco, California.*

What's in a Name?

This style had its origins in England, under the influence of architect Richard Norman Shaw (1831–1912). The name "Queen Anne" is perhaps misleading, since popular architecture during this queen's reign (1702–14) was dominated by a more formal, Renaissance-inspired style. In developing the prototypical English version of the Queen Anne brick house, Shaw and others drew upon Tudor architectural models, adding details like oriel windows and corner towers.

Machine-Age Architecture

The Queen Anne style was propelled to its zenith in the United States and Canada by the advent of the industrial machine age, which allowed for factory-made, precut architectural details that were transported economically via the rapidly expanding railroad system. Suddenly, people all across the continent, including those in rural areas, wanted the fancy houses that they saw in the popular pattern books that were being disseminated at the time, which often featured circular corner towers and other features commonly associated with Queen Anne architecture. Patterned shingles, spindles, and finials were sometimes added; the most elaborately ornamented Queen Anne homes may be known as "Eastlake," "gingerbread," or the polychromatic "painted ladies." In Queen Anne homes where masonry, rather than wood, was used as the primary construction material, decorative stone, brick, and terra-cotta patterns are seen, with little or no wooden ornamentation. Other Queen Anne homes are half-timbered, with exposed wood framing. In these homes, the spaces between the timbers may be filled with plaster, stone, or even brick.

CHARLES LOCKE EASTLAKE

The term "Eastlake" refers to a style of ornamentation. It was named for English interior designer and architect Charles Locke Eastlake (1833–1906), a critic of the Gothic Revival style. He favored "simple, elegant motifs" rather than the extravagant excesses that would later become associated with his name—much to his dismay. His 1868 book on home design was extremely popular and influential, especially in the United States, but his preference for understated design was soon forgotten by those who enthusiastically decorated their homes with the newly available factory-made, precut building materials.

SHINGLE STYLE

A Shingle-style house is so named for its typically uniform covering of thin wooden shingles, usually cedar, that were stained instead of painted. This style, primarily a trend in residential architecture, emerged in New England, where it echoed house styles dating from the early colonial period.

A Victorian Anomaly

The Shingle style's lack of lavish ornamentation places it in stark contrast to most Victorian housing styles, and the birth of the style marked a significant shift in the architecture of the American home. In comparison to other late-nineteenth-century homes, Shingle houses have a more rustic, informal, and relaxed feel. However, many Shingle homes were built to a large, rambling floor plan and have irregular massing and spacious verandahs—features that are similar to those of other Victorian housing styles.

Seaside Cottages

Although they appear rustic and simple, many Shingle-style homes were originally built as vacation cottages for the wealthy.

ABOVE: *The Edna Villa (built 1882–83), by McKim, Mead, and White, in fashionable Newport, Rhode Island.*

OPPOSITE: *The William G. Low House, Bristol, Rhode Island.*

WILLIAM G. LOW HOUSE

Location: Bristol, Rhode Island.
Date: 1887.
Architects: McKim, Mead, and White.
Materials: Wood frame; Covered in straight-cut cypress shingles.
Significance: The form of this oceanside house (which no longer stands) was completely dominated by its roof; the entire structure has a pleasingly simple, yet bold, triangular shape.

They were first built in New England seaside resorts like Newport, Rhode Island; Cape Cod, Massachusetts; along the Maine coast; and in Eastern Long Island. The style soon spread to affluent neighborhoods around the country. Architects H.H. Richardson and McKim, Mead, and White designed a number of renowned Shingle dwellings, and even Frank Lloyd Wright was inspired by the Shingle style in his early designs.

Back in Fashion

The Shingle style waned around the start of the twentieth century, but it enjoyed a rebirth in the latter half of the century. In the 1960s, architect Robert Venturi built a Shingle-style home for his mother in Chestnut Hill, Pennsylvania. Another architect, Robert Stern, designed a Long Island home after a Shingle-style dwelling from the 1880s. Today, the rustic look is back in fashion, and there are many homes being built that utilize key elements of the original Shingle style.

RICHARDSONIAN ROMANESQUE

In the late nineteenth century, American architect Henry Hobson Richardson began to propagate the Romanesque Revival style—but he also adapted the style a good deal, resulting in a distinctive new look that became his trademark.

STYLE FILE

Notable Features:
Massive rounded arches;
Deeply recessed windows
   and entryways;
Short piers;
Rusticated masonry;
Domes;
Circular towers with coni-
   cal "witch's cap" roofs;
Asymmetrical facades;
Decorative wall patterns;
Windows paired or in
   groups of three;
Stone transoms and
   polychrome lintels;
Parapeted dormers.

Major Influences:
Romanesque Revival.

Where and When:
The United States;
   c. 1870–1900.

Richardson's Contribution

Richardson was educated in Paris, France, and influenced by architects and historical buildings in both Europe and America. His buildings were characterized by massive rounded arches, deeply recessed windows and doors, short wooden or stone piers (instead of columns), and, sometimes, fantastical circular towers topped with conical "witch's cap" roofs. The overall impression is of a solid, "squat" shape, emphasized by the use of large blocks of rusticated stone. Examples of Richardson's designs can be seen in Trinity Church in Boston (1872), regarded as a masterpiece of American architecture, and the John Glessner House in Chicago (1885). Even today, he is considered one of the greatest architects in U.S. history.

OPPOSITE: *Richardson's Trinity Church, Copley Square, in the Back Bay area of Boston, Massachusetts.*

RIGHT: *Detail of the massive, arched entryway of Harvard University's Austin Hall (H.H. Richardson, 1881–84), Cambridge, Massachusetts.*

Successors to Richardson

Despite the style's name, there were other well-known architects who designed buildings in the Richardsonian fashion, including Charles F. McKim and John Wellborn Root. The Amelia S. Givin Public Library in Mt. Holly Springs, Pennsylvania (1890), designed by noted Pittsburgh architect James T. Steen, is considered one of the finest examples of the Richardsonian style, as is the Inner Quad Arcade (Shepley, Rutan, and Coolidge, 1891) at Stanford University, Palo Alto, California. Richardson's legacy is also evident in the work of Louis Sullivan and the Chicago School.

TRINITY CHURCH

Location: Boston, Massachusetts.
Date: 1872–77.
Architect: Henry Hobson Richardson.
Materials: Granite ashlar, brownstone facing, terra cotta.
Significance: Trinity Church is the building that stands out in U.S. architectural history as having most singularly established an architect and a style.

EXOTIC REVIVAL

The Exotic Revivals were inspired by, and expressed in, various Asian and Islamic styles, some of which were popularized by French archeological work in Egypt during Napoleon's campaigns. In Europe and the United States, these styles were adapted to the design of contemporary public buildings, as well as expensive private homes, beginning in the early nineteenth century.

STYLE FILE

Notable Features:
Egyptian Revival:
  Battered walls; fluted
  columns with lotus or
  palm capitals; concave
  cornices; winged-disk
  motifs.
Oriental Revival: S-curve
  (ogee) arches; onion-
  shaped, Turkish-style
  domes; geometric
  masonry patterns.
Moorish Revival: Moorish
  arches; domes of
  various sizes and
  shapes; minaret-style
  spires; mosaic and tile
  surface decorations.

Major Influences:
Asian styles;
Islamic styles.

Where and When:
Western Europe, North
  America; c. 1810–1930.

BELOW: *The Exotic Revival Templeton Carpet Factory in Glasgow, Scotland (1888–92, after Venice's Doges' Palace).*

An Unconventional Style

Called "exotic," these Eastern and Mideastern architectural forms were something of a fad in Western European and American architecture, quite at odds with the styles in vogue in the Western world at the time. Therefore, to build one's house, palace, or fanciful folly in these elaborate and expensive Exotic styles was both a show of wealth and a defiance of convention. John Nash's design for the Royal Pavilion (1815–23, *see* page 153) in the English coastal town of Brighton was one such example, which combined elaborate Chinese and Islamic forms and motifs.

Eclectic Diversity

Exotic Revival architecture mirrored a romantic interest in history and archeology. In the United States, it was not uncommon for Exotic-style details to be superimposed upon typical, cube-shaped Italianate houses. A number of synagogues were also built in Moorish styles, recalling Moorish-influenced synagogues built in medieval times in Spain.

ABOVE: *Dohány Synagogue, 1854–59, Budapest, Hungary.*

OPPOSITE: *Polychrome brick patterns and ogee arches are among the details that identify this Moorish-style Florida mansion as an Exotic Revival building.*

LEFT: *Olana, New York State. Artist Frederic Church commissioned Calvert Vaux to design this Hudson Valley landmark (1874). With its whimsical towers, striking archways, polychrome stenciling, and 250 acres of scenic grounds within view of the Catskill Mountains, this Persian-style home is probably the best-known example of the Exotic Revival style in the United States.*

BEAUX ARTS

This style, which is characterized by the extravagant use of Classical elements, is named for the legendary *École des Beaux-Arts* in Paris, France, where some of the best-known European and American architects studied at around the turn of the twentieth century. The term *beaux arts* is French for "fine art."

Classical Meets Renaissance

Also known as "Beaux Arts Classicism," or "Academic Classicism," this style combines Classical design aesthetics with Renaissance ideals. The *École des Beaux-Arts* stressed the study of Greek and Roman structures, and the main principles of the Beaux Arts style are order, symmetry, formality, grandiosity, and elaborate ornamentation. The doctrines and teachings of this school dominated French architecture from the seventeenth until the early twentieth century. An abhorrence of undecorated surfaces (or *horror vacui*) is one characteristic of its teachings—a principle that also guided architects who created works in the Second Empire style.

STYLE FILE

Notable Features:
Grandiose compositions;
Symmetrical facades;
Projecting facades or
  pavilions with arches;
Colossal columns, often
  paired, and pilasters;
Balconies;
Finely detailed decoration
  (medallions, swags, car-
  touches, and statuary);
Stone finishing;
Grand stairwells;
Windows framed by
  columns or balustrades;
Triangular pediments;
Pronounced cornices and
  entablatures topped
  with a tall parapet,
  balustrade, or attic.

Major Influences:
Classical buildings.

Where and When:
Europe, North America;
1885–1925.

Public to Private

Many of the great exhibitions—including those held in Philadelphia (1876), Chicago (1893), and St. Louis (1904)—featured Beaux Arts structures that rocketed this style to immense popularity. In Europe and in North America, the earliest Beaux Arts designs were generally reserved for grand and colossal public structures like museums, railroad stations, banks, libraries, memorials, courthouses, and government and municipal buildings.

Though Beaux Arts began as the preferred style for grand public structures, wealthy citizens soon adopted the lavish style for the design of their own private mansions. In the United States, there were entire neighborhoods designed in the Beaux Arts style, with massive, opulent houses, wide thoroughfares, and vast green spaces. The popularity of the style began to decrease in the 1920s; twenty-five years later, these buildings were considered pretentious and showy. Later in the twentieth century, however, a new crop of Postmodern architects rediscovered an appreciation of the Beaux Arts principles.

ABOVE: *The landmark Union Station in Washington, D.C. (interior detail, inset image).*
OPPOSITE, TOP: *Interior detail of the imposing, domed chapel at Annapolis Military Academy.*
OPPOSITE, BELOW: *Period view of Central Station, Milan, Italy; the building was seriously damaged during World War II.*

CHATEAUESQUE

With its epic scale and lavish stone construction, the Chateauesque style was well suited for the opulent country mansions of the wealthy. These structures were usually built of marble or limestone, and, unlike many other Victorian styles, the sheer size of these stately homes precluded cheaper reproductions.

LEFT: *The Biltmore Estate, Asheville, North Carolina, built for George W. Vanderbilt by hundreds of workers between 1888 and 1895.*

STYLE FILE

Notable Features:
Steeply pitched hipped or gabled roofs with multiple vertical adornments;
Relief-sculptured gables;
Multiple dormers;
Belt courses;
Conical "candle-snuffer" roof towers;
Tall, ornamented, corbeled chimneys;
Numerous balconies;
Corbeled brackets;
Semicircular arches;
Pilasters;
Paired cross-windows, or arched windows;
Gothic tracery;
Gothic finials.

Major Influences:
French Renaissance;
Gothic.

Where and When:
Europe, North America; c. 1860–1910.

Gothic and Renaissance Influences

The easily recognizable Chateauesque style combined Gothic elements with Renaissance details found in sixteenth-century French chateaus (*see* page 81). Though luxurious, the Chateauesque style has a rustic, yet forbidding, look—and, in fact, most Chateauesque homes are found in isolated, rural locations, both in Europe and in the United States.

Ostentatious Affluence

Many affluent patrons who commissioned designs for such mansions expressed a desire to eclipse, or outdo, the lavish homes of their equally well-off neighbors. Often cited as a prime example of this is the famous Biltmore

ABOVE: *Hecker House, Detroit.*
BELOW, RIGHT: *Château Frontenac Hôtel, Quebec.*

A SMALL PIECE OF FRANCE

The Hecker House (above) in Detroit, Michigan, designed by Louis Kamper, was built in 1888–91 for a local notable who wanted his home modeled on the Château Chenonceau (pictured below) in France's Loire Valley.

Estate, which was designed for George W. Vanderbilt by Richard Morris Hunt (*see also* pages 154–55). Other notable American architects of similar mansions included Daniel Burnham and John Wellborn Root.

The popularity of the Chateauesque style began to fade not long after Hunt's death in 1895. At around the turn of the century, inventions like the automobile, electricity, and the telephone had rapidly begun to transform the lives of Westerners. A more informal lifestyle began to emerge, replacing the rigid formality embodied in Victorian tastes.

SECOND EMPIRE

Houses and public buildings in the Second Empire style were modeled on the rich Baroque Revival that flourished during the rebuilding of Paris, France, supervised by Baron Haussmann in the reign of Napoleon III (1852–70, the Second Empire).

STYLE FILE

Notable Features:
High mansard roofs with rounded cornices;
Wrought-iron cresting;
Dormer windows projecting from the attic;
Brackets below eaves, balconies, and bays;
Cupolas;
Patterned slate roofs;
Classical pediments and paired columns;
Tall first-story windows;
Small entry porches.

Major Influences:
Baroque;
Italianate;
French Renaissance;
Italian Renaissance.

Where and When:
Western Europe and North America;
c. 1855–85.

Paris on Display

The Second Empire style is generally highly ornamented, which is why critics apply to it the term *horror vacui*, or the fear of empty space (or unadorned surfaces). The Louvre, remodeled 1852–57, is one of the famous Parisian examples of this style, which rapidly became fashionable elsewhere in Europe and in North America. While many Second Empire buildings are large-scale ornate public and residential structures built of stone (*see* page 187), the style was also popular for domestic architecture, sometimes of wood.

RIGHT: *The opulent Philadelphia, Pennsylvania, City Hall, built 1871–1901. At more than 500 feet tall, this is one of the tallest masonry structures in the world. The roof is crowned with an imposing statue of William Penn.*

The Mansard Profile

Imagine the haunted houses that loom upon lonely hilltops in a multitude of Hollywood horror movies, including Alfred Hitchcock's *Psycho*, and you've got the classic Second Empire house. Because of its tall mansard roof (which has a distinctive profile) and its elaborate wrought-iron cresting, a mansard mansion is likely to appear forbidding and spooky. However, this is not at all how these homes were viewed in their heyday, when they were considered quite stylish, modern, and majestic. The fact that these homes could be built in a tall, narrow shape made them particularly attractive for city building on small lots in the nineteenth century.

ABOVE: *Glen Auburn Mansion in Natchez, Mississippi, has a concave mansard roof.*

BELOW: *A view of the Louvre, Paris, photographed soon after its Second Empire remodeling.*

STEAMBOAT GOTHIC

This style, a whimsical offshoot of Carpenter Gothic, was inspired by the elegance and opulence of the River Road. A Steamboat Gothic house is resplendent with gingerbread scrollwork, latticework, and trellises—like the fancy steamboats that were once a frequent sight on the Ohio and Mississippi Rivers.

STYLE FILE

Notable Features:
Pointed, steep intersecting
  Gothic gables;
Cupolas and towers;
Battlements;
Asymmetrical floor plan;
Opulent appliqué work,
  finials, bargeboards,
  balustrades, stickwork,
  and moldings;
Gingerbread scrollwork,
  latticework, and trellises;
Intricate paintwork;
Emphasized verticality;
Grand wraparound
  porches and verandahs;
Metal "smokestack"
  chimneys.

Major Influences:
Carpenter Gothic;
Georgian;
Queen Anne.

Where and When:
North America;
  c. 1850–90.

From Boats to Homes

The earliest steamboats were utilitarian craft, made simply to transport goods and passengers swiftly to their destinations. However, following the expansion of the U.S. railroad system during the Civil War, the riverboats faced new competition. Steamboat companies responded by commissioning larger, lavishly appointed vessels that incorporated elaborate Victorian architectural elements and—much like today's luxury cruise ships—featured not only private cabins for wealthy passengers, but elegant staterooms and dining facilities, so that the boats resembled floating palaces. The Steamboat Gothic style borrowed features from these ships, resulting in elaborately detailed houses that evoked the opulence of the plantation-owner's lifestyle. Craftsmen carved delicate embellishments for the towers and gables, while wraparound prowlike verandahs and "smokestack" chimneys added to the steamboat look.

ABOVE: *The eclectic San Francisco Plantation, Louisiana.*
LEFT: *The Jackson House at Reynolds Plantation, Georgia, a Queen Anne Steamboat Gothic.*

Gothic or Not?

Some commentators use this label interchangeably with Carpenter Gothic, but the pointed gables and other hallmark features of the Gothic style are not evident in all buildings that have been called Steamboat Gothic. The unifying themes are elaborate detailing and a resemblance to the River Road craft.

OPPOSITE: *The Mark Twain House, Hartford, Connecticut, has a shiplike shape, abundant decorative details, and "smoke- stack" chimneys. It was built in 1874 of brick with wood trim.*
BELOW: *An Octagonal-style house in Hudson, Wisconsin.*

THE OCTAGONAL FAD

The steamboat was not the only unusual Victorian Gothic shape variation. Orson Squire Fowler (1809–87) conceived of octagonal homes and detailed his suggested construction methods in *The Octagon House: A Home for All* (1848). According to Fowler, they were cheap to build, had economy of space, were easier to heat, and remained cool in the summertime. Having eight sides and (often) a cupola, he also pointed out that these homes offered much better views than conventional houses.

URBAN APARTMENTS

The nineteenth century was an era of industrial growth for many nations, and with economic expansion came urbanization and the concomitant need for denser housing in the cities that experienced rapid growth. The only way was up.

STYLE FILE

Notable Features:
Masonry construction of stone or brick;
Concrete (Portland cement) in use from the 1850s in Europe;
Five to seven stories;
Unified appearance of newly designed streets;
Balconies, cornices, and ornamental features in harmonious patterns.

Major Influences:
Construction technology;
Materials availability;
City growth and planning.

Where and When:
Western Europe and North America; from the 1850s onward.

ABOVE: *Fire escapes on a row of New York City apartments. Many such early buildings have apartments facing either to the front or rear, with windows to one side only. French design influenced the layout and structure of large apartment buildings in New York in the later part of the century, with central courtyards allowing for windows looking inward as well as to the street. The eight-story Dakota Building (1880–84) is a notable example.*

A Tale of Several Cities

As the capital city of empire, London was the world's largest city through the nineteenth century. With a population of a million by 1800, it already had entire neighborhoods of Georgian residential architecture, and it grew steadily rather than in a single explosion. But other British cities—Glasgow, Liverpool, and Manchester—grew rapidly, as did other centers of trade and commerce. By mid-century, Paris had around 900,000 residents, and New York City had overtaken Philadelphia as the largest U.S. city, with half a million residents. Governments responded to the sudden demand for housing in different ways.

LEFT: *The late-Victorian St. George's Mansions, Glasgow, built by the City Improvement Trust as high-quality housing. Glasgow's Victorian tenement buildings were constructed of sandstone—either red, as here, or honey-colored ("blond")—up to five stories in height.*

CAST IRON

In the 1850s, New York architect James Bogardus (see page 190) led the charge in designing with cast iron, which was cheap and plentiful; not only was it supportive, but it could be decorative. SoHo's cast-iron district was commercial, but it was opened up to residential zoning in the 1970s, when artists rushed in to renovate the spaces as loft apartments. For safety, however, these buildings had long been fortified with masonry, because cast iron had proven catastrophically unsafe, buckling in fire.

City Planning

During the "Second Empire" (1852–70), the layout of Paris was transformed by Baron Georges Haussmann (*see* pages 182–83), and the new plan included relatively upscale dwellings in the city center. Many blocks of stone-built apartments were constructed, with elegant balconies, cornices, and mansard roofs. In New York, brownstone rowhouses were built for the better off, but from 1839, multi-story, walk-up tenements sprang up in the Lower East Side to cope with rapid population growth. Initially of poor quality, regulations soon drove up standards; luxury apartment buildings were constructed from the 1870s.

RIGHT: *Rue Monge, Paris: a Haussmann apartment building with decorative stonework and other detailing typical of the new-look city streets.*

TUDOR REVIVAL

Tudor-style homes (*see* pages 84–85, also referred to as "Old English") enjoyed a Victorian-era revival in Britain's growing suburbs and, at the same time, found popularity in Continental Europe and the United States, where the style endured until the 1920s. The style is easily identified by half-timbering and a rustic mix of stone or brick with stucco and wood, and (usually) steep roofs and gables.

STYLE FILE

Notable Features:
Half-timbering;
Steeply pitched roofs;
Prominent cross-gables;
Grouped, leaded windows
  with small panes;
Tall chimneys, often
  with decorative pots;
Mix of stone or brick with
  stucco and wood;
Asymmetrical plan.

Major Influences:
English Tudor.

Where and When:
North America, Europe;
c. 1880–1940s, 1970–85.

Suburban Picturesque

More broadly, the revival of the old-fashioned Tudor cottage, with its rural connotations, may be thought of as part of the romantically nostalgic Victorian trend against urban living and the fast pace of industrialization. Though evocative of the old English country house, the Tudor Revival was a largely suburban phenomenon. Houses in this style span areas of the suburban neighborhoods of the U.S. Northeast and Midwest, as well as English cities. And, in pleasing contrast with many of the other, more formal, Victorian revival styles, the form and material of Tudor homes lend them a tendency to merge attractively with the natural landscape.

LEFT: *A Tudor Revival–style house in a U.S. suburb, with typical features including half-timbering and steep gables.*

BELOW: *Detail of a street in Chester, England, which has an old center with Jacobean buildings and Victorian-era half-timbered structures, many designed by John Douglas.*

OPPOSITE: *Pewabic Pottery, in Detroit, Michigan, combines the Tudor Revival style with English Arts and Crafts features.*

PEWABIC POTTERY

Location: Detroit, Michigan.
Date: 1907.
Architects: William B. Stratton and Frank D. Baldwin.
Materials: Brick, stucco, and wood.
Significance: Stratton and Baldwin designed this English Tudor-style pottery building as a crafts center rather than a factory. Elaborately constructed and decorated, the half-timbered building has a steeply pitched roof, a rustic-looking facade, and large chimneys. Pewabic Pottery has changed very little since 1907, and the original cabinets, tables, clay-working machine, and dumb waiter are still in use by ceramicists. It was designated a National Historic Landmark in 1991.

From City to Resort

In the United States, "Tudor Revival" also refers to a regional English cottage style known as the Cotswold Cottage, which imitates cottages built since medieval times in the Cotswold region of England. These were originally built of honey-colored Cotswold limestone and had steeply pitched, thatched roofs. Their popularity in America peaked around the 1920s; these charming homes often have a "mock-thatched" roof of slate or cedar, large chimneys, an uneven sloping roofline, small window panes, and short doors.

The Tudor Revival and Cotswold Cottage styles saw a brief comeback in the 1940s. Then, after another disappearance from the scene, there was renewed interest in Europe and North America in the nostalgic 1970s and '80s.

"IRON AGE" MATERIALISM

Not only did new, mechanized methods of manufacture and mass production herald the use of industrial materials like cast and wrought iron in nineteenth-century architecture, but many of the structures of which they were fundamental components were built in response to the demands of the machine age.

BELOW: *The iron-and-glass Palm House (1844–48) at Kew Gardens, London.*

Early Cast-Iron Constructions

In Britain, several iron bridges (notably that at Coalbrookdale, Shropshire, raised by Abraham Darby between 1777 and 1779) and iron-framed, fireproof textile mills served as prototypes for many cast-iron structures that sprang up during the nineteenth century. Cast-iron stanchions, wrought-iron beams, and, from the 1840s, plate glass having proved easily manufactured, strong, and durable, all that remained was the development of a style that perfectly complemented these materials' qualities.

Crystal Palaces

Although increasingly used in commercial buildings, such as the Classically influenced, cast-iron facades of New York City constructions by James Bogardus (1800–74), the combination of cast iron and glass found its most influential expression in conservatories, one of the most acclaimed being Kew Garden's Palm House, London, designed by Decimus Burton

METAL MARVELS

Imitation expresses admiration, and that the Old World could still impress the New World was demonstrated in 1853, when New York raised its own Crystal Palace (below). The original comprised 2,150 iron girders, 3,300 iron columns, and nearly 300,000 panes of glass. Once the Great Exhibition was over, it was swiftly dismantled and reconstructed south of the River Thames, in Sydenham, where it remained until fire destroyed it in 1936. Another nineteenth-century metal marvel survives, however, namely the Eiffel Tower in Paris, France, which Gustave Eiffel (1832–1923) designed to be both the entrance arch and high point of the *Exposition Universelle* (Universal Exhibition) of 1889. At 986 feet, this cast-iron skeletal tower was the world's tallest manmade construction at that time.

(1800–81) and Richard Turner. Joseph Paxton (1801–65) also designed an impressive conservatory at Chatsworth, a large country estate, between 1836 and 1840, but it was his 1,800-foot-long Crystal Palace that was hailed as a cast-iron triumph. Created for Britain's Great Exhibition of 1851, this showcase glasshouse was the first building whose components were prefabricated before being rapidly assembled on site in London's Hyde Park. From these inspirational glasshouses developed the iron-and-glass domes, vaults, and canopies that later enclosed many Western cities' railroad stations, reading rooms, and shopping arcades.

ARTS AND CRAFTS (ENGLISH)

This style of architecture was largely inspired by the Utopian ideals of two Englishmen, John Ruskin (1819–1900, *see also* page 158) and William Morris (1834–96), who believed that living among handmade objects of natural materials would have a humanizing effect on society.

STYLE FILE

Notable Features:
Local stone and brick;
Rustic, stone-dressed
  doorways and windows;
Open porches;
Projecting eaves;
Overhanging rafters;
Large windows with
  leaded-glass decoration;
Large, square chimneys;
Exposed construction
  (pegs in beams, bare
  stone and brick);
Intricate, crafted joints;
Asymmetrical plan.

Major Influences:
Gothic buildings;
William Morris;
John Ruskin.

Where and When:
England; c. 1880–1910.

BELOW: *Morris's Red House, 1859, designed by Philip Webb.*

Simplicity in Living

Ruskin and Morris sought to counteract the "soulless" impersonality of the machine age in which they lived, and to promote craftsmanship over the mass production of the industrial era. Morris in particular was a proponent of simple living: his dictum "Possess nothing you do not know to be useful or believe to be beautiful" popularized the desire for a simpler, more natural, and egalitarian lifestyle. Both men looked back to medieval times, when craftsmen took pride in their work and created thoughtfully designed objects of natural, rather than synthetic, materials that were inherently beautiful. It was also important that the construction materials were locally sourced, so that the building could blend, or be "in harmony," with its surroundings. Ironically, though both men espoused socialist ideals, the objects that they and their like-minded colleagues created were expensive and out of the reach of ordinary working people.

Design Unity

The principle of unity in design was central to the Arts and Crafts movement: it applied not only to buildings, but to their furnishings and fittings, as well as to ambient landscapes and gardens. Each new building, with its interior and surroundings, was seen as an integrated project. Space was carefully planned to reclaim "dead," unused areas like hallways.

Precursors to Modern Design

At around the turn of the twentieth century, the philosophy of Ruskin and Morris began to catch the attention of architects around the world. In the United States, they were influential in the Craftsman, Mission, and Rustic styles and Frank Lloyd Wright's early works (*see* pages 204–211), while in Europe, the Art and Crafts movement helped inspire the Celtic Revival (*see* pages 198–99) and the Art Nouveau and Secession styles (*see* pages 212–15). Their principal tenets of functionality and organic, sustainable methods and materials are still highly influential today, and are seen in many of the trends in contemporary architecture (*see* the last chapter of this book).

ABOVE: *Standen, Sussex, England, designed by Philip Webb, built 1891–94.*

STANDEN

Location: Sussex, England.
Date: 1891–94.
Architect: Philip Webb.
Materials: Sandstone (quarried from the site), local bricks, hanging tiles, and oak weather-boarding.
Significance: Webb was a leading architect of the Arts and Crafts movement in England, and Standen was one of his finest masterpieces. He designed not only the house itself, but also the interior fittings —everything from the fireplaces to the electrical outlets—as well as some of the furniture. The house and property (including terraced gardens) is now owned by the National Trust.

EARLY MODERN ARCHITECTURE

The foundations of Modernism in architecture were laid during the Victorian era, with industrialization and new technology setting the pace for change. Commercial, social, and demographic factors played their part, too. The skyscraper was born as a result of technological advances combining to provide a solution to the increasing pressure on space in thriving cities: build upward! Many consider Louis Henri Sullivan's boldly innovative Chicago School structures to be the first expression of Modernism in architecture. Others claim that Modern architecture was born in Europe, not in the form of the advanced engineering of commercial buildings, but in the philosophy of those young radicals (including the Secessionists Adolf Loos and Otto Wagner) who scorned adornment and advocated instead a purity of form. In fact, Modernism in architecture rapidly took on a wide variety of meanings and manifested itself in many different visual modes, as may be seen in the following pages.

OPPOSITE: *Cass Gilbert's Woolworth Building (1913), New York City, represented the latest technology and was the world's tallest building when it was built. With its Gothic Revival appearance, it is a landmark that combines historicism with Modernism.*

AMERICAN RENAISSANCE

The American Renaissance, named for a richly artistic period in the United States rather than a European Renaissance aesthetic, straddled the Victorian and early Modern eras, both chronologically and in stylistic terms.

STYLE FILE

Notable Features:
Monumental scale;
Classical themes and
 features;
Marble and other lavish,
 imposing masonry;
Modern lines, especially
 verticals;
Use of new technologies;
Broad, open spaces,
 malls, and boulevards;
Parks and gardens.

Major Influences:
Beaux Arts;
Classical revivals;
Industry and technology.

Where and When:
Major U.S. cities;
1880–1915.

National Pride

Partially coinciding with the "gilded age," this was a self-confident and wealthy period in American history—for the great barons, at least—and a time of unprecedented industrial growth and economic expansion. The artists and architects of the movement were intensely nationalistic; they were optimistic, too, about a future that they believed would be determined by technological innovation and a democratic, capitalist system. Influenced by Classical styles and Beaux Arts architecture, but also by the first flowering of Modernism, architects like Stanford White, Richard Morris Hunt, and Charles Follen McKim created monuments, parks, and imposing civic buildings—and extravagant residences for the power brokers.

OPPOSITE, ABOVE: *The subject of this mosaic by Elihu Vedder in the Library of Congress is the Roman goddess of wisdom, Minerva, whose image graces several buildings of this era.*
RIGHT: *Richard Morris Hunt, architect of the Biltmore Estate, designed the pedestal for the Statue of Liberty.*
OPPOSITE, BELOW: *The opening of New York's Brooklyn Bridge, the world's first steel-wire suspension bridge, in 1883 heralded the beginning of the American Renaissance.*

**THE BOSTON
PUBLIC LIBRARY**

Location: Copley Square, Boston, Massachusetts.
Date: 1887–95.
Architect: Charles Follen McKim.
Materials: Sandstone, with marble detailing.
Significance: The monumental scale, elegant lines, grand arches, and Classical proportions of this landmark, combined with the lofty tone of its inscriptions and carvings of artists, scientists, and statesmen, earned it a reputation as America's first great expression of civic art.

The "City Beautiful"

The architects of the World's Columbian Exhibition (1893) in Chicago, as well as city planners designing Washington, D.C., Denver, and other cities, created uplifting new environments that were characterized by their sheer grandeur, with expansive public spaces, inspiring monuments, and nationalistic motifs celebrating American history and the national values of liberty, rationalism, and progress.

CELTIC REVIVAL

The Celtic Revival in architecture can be traced to late-nineteenth-century Scotland, then in the midst of a renaissance of Celtic traditions, and specifically to the work of one innovative and unusually talented Scotsman.

STYLE FILE

Notable Features:
Heavy masonry walls;
Art Nouveau motifs;
Modern materials and
  techniques (large, indus-
  trial, braced windows);
Pale colors;
Rectilinear styles;
Vertical forms;
Simple, functional struc-
  tures and spaces;
Mixture of rational,
  restrained forms and
  stylized ornamentation.

Major Influences:
Scottish tradition;
English Arts and Crafts;
Japanese designs.

Where and When:
Scotland and Ireland;
  c. 1889–1913.

ABOVE AND OPPOSITE:
The Glasgow School of Art.
BELOW: *Stylized carvings in the Glasgow School style, as seen in the work of Mackintosh and Margaret Macdonald.*

Charles Rennie Mackintosh

The Glasgow architect, artist, and designer Charles Rennie Mackintosh (1868–1928) studied at the Glasgow School of Art, where he and his colleagues were influenced by the nascent Art Nouveau movement (*see* pages 212–13), with its slender, undulating curves and subtle, opalescent colors. Mackintosh went on to develop what became known as the Celtic Revival style by merging an eclectic blend of influences together with his own inventions. In addition to Art Nouveau, these influences included Scottish Baronial architecture (*see* pages 77 and 157) and other European and Japanese designs. In his designs, Mackintosh drew heavily on traditional Celtic architecture and ornamentation

THE GLASGOW SCHOOL OF ART

Location: Glasgow, Scotland.

Date: 1897–1909.

Architect: C.R. Mackintosh.

Significance: When Mackintosh won a competition to design this building for his alma mater, it was his first commission. It is now recognized as the most important building of his career. At the time of its construction, this austere, towering, rectangular structure was highly controversial because of its severity, its asymmetrical facade, and its lack of Classical elements or sculptural decoration. Today, it is one of the world's best-known buildings, and is considered by many to mark the beginning of Modern architecture.

—especially that of Scottish castles and baronial mansions. His Glasgow School of Art evokes castle architecture in its massive walls and irregularly placed, narrow fenestration.

Modern Simplicity

Mackintosh preferred to work with modern construction materials and techniques, as seen in his large, braced industrial windows and his innovative use of electric lighting. He also believed that "construction should be decorated, and not decoration constructed"—i.e., that a building's ornamentation should be connected to its functional, structural features, such as its brackets or roof trusses. He designed the Glasgow School of Art from the inside out, meaning that the functionality of the interior spaces defined the building's overall appearance from the outside. The resulting structure is immensely simple, functional, and logical, with all of its varied elements fused together in an eclectic harmony.

THE CHICAGO SCHOOL

As the twentieth century dawned, a group of Chicago-based architects, most notably Louis Henri Sullivan, created a new style of tall commercial buildings, enabled by important technological innovations and a bold, radical approach.

BELOW: *The floral-motif decorative panels that adorn the Wainwright Building exemplify the Chicago School's distinctive exterior ornamentation.*

New Materials, New Heights

Several factors contributed to the new style emerging in Chicago. The development of steel-frame and cast-iron technology made possible a supporting structure lighter than solid masonry, while crucial advances were made in understanding both fire safety and stability in storm conditions. Architects and engineers were now free to plan much taller buildings, without compromising safety, and the newly invented elevator enabled convenience.

Founding Fathers

William Le Baron Jenney is often described as the father of this school: he designed the first tall building (1883–85) supported entirely by a skeleton of iron and steel. Louis Sullivan began his career in Jenney's office, later (in 1871) joining the firm of Dankmar Adler, beginning a fifteen-year partnership that would result in some of the most prominent, ambitious, and original buildings of their generation.

THE WAINWRIGHT BUILDING

Location: St. Louis, Missouri.
Date: 1890–92.
Architect: Louis Sullivan.
Materials: Steel frame, terra-cotta cladding.
Significance: Sullivan's masterpiece is generally regarded as the first modern skyscraper and a landmark that defined the Chicago School's style. Unornamented at street level and with an explicit grid of vertical piers and horizontal stories above, it is decorated with exquisitely carved panels that give the building a restrained beauty. It revolutionized American architecture.

The Chicago Style

Adler and Sullivan's buildings were characterized by the use of steel or cast-iron framing with masonry cladding—often of terra cotta—columnar (or rectangular) in shape and ornamented in a restrained, yet original, style incorporating naturalistic motifs. These were carved on panels placed on the facades and on the deep cornices framing the flat roofs. While the carvings had an Art Nouveau flavor, the ornamentation was discreet, sometimes scarcely visible, from a distance, when only the frame's shape was evident. Their best-known works include the Wainwright Building (1890–92, St. Louis), the Carson, Pirie, Scott Department Store (1904, Chicago), and the Security (formerly National Farmers') Bank (1908, Owatonna, Minnesota). Another prominent feature of the style was the tripartite "Chicago window," which consisted of a large central pane flanked by two narrower, sash-hung windows.

ABOVE: *The Wainwright Building, St. Louis, Missouri.*

BELOW: *Floral decoration detail on the facade of Sullivan's Security (National Farmer's) Bank, Owatonna, Minnesota.*

SKYSCRAPERS

Until the late nineteenth century, architects' lofty ambitions were limited by existing building materials and conventions. Increasing industrialization—and particularly the strides made in manufacturing steel, concrete, and plate glass—changed all that, however: the sky is no longer the limit.

Rising from the Ashes

The skyscraper was born in Chicago, Illinois, where devastation by fire in 1871 meant that the city had to be rebuilt. The escalating cost of land prompted smaller footprints for new buildings. The skyscraper style—pioneered by Holabird & Roche in their twenty-two-story Tacoma Building (1887–8), Louis Sullivan, and fellow members of the Chicago School—was predicated on the steel skeleton frame, which had the significant advantages of being strong, relatively light, and fireproof.

RIGHT: *Iconic landmarks of North Michigan Avenue, Chicago: the Wrigley Building (1920–24) and the neo-Gothic Tribune Tower (1923–25).*

RIGHT: *Louis Sullivan's 17-story Schiller Building, or Garrick Theater, Chicago (1892, demolished in 1961).*
BELOW: *The Flatiron Building (1902), designed by Daniel Burnham and formerly called the Fuller Building, stands on a narrow lot at the junction of Broadway and Fifth Avenue in Manhattan, New York.*

New York, New York

New York City's skyline became famous for its skyscrapers, the first including the quirky Flatiron Building (1902), designed by Daniel Burnham, and the Gothic-style Woolworth Building (1913), by Cass Gilbert. The Art Deco years contributed many further such iconic profiles, notably the Chrysler and Empire State buildings (see pages 221–23).

Early Skyscraper Features

As the world's richest capitalist nation, America led the way in skyscraper construction, but wherever they were raised, and whichever architectural style they conformed to, most Early Modern skyscrapers had certain common features: steel or reinforced-concrete frames, repetitive fenestration, later often incorporated into plate-glass curtain walls, and, of course, breathtaking heights.

PRAIRIE STYLE

Frank Lloyd Wright was the creator of this enduring style: he sought to design buildings to suit the wide, open spaces of the Midwestern landscape, rejecting the Classical revivals that were then popular, turning to Japan for inspiration.

STYLE FILE

Notable Features:
Horizontal planes and
  rectilinear forms;
Broad eaves;
Large, cantilevered
  terraces and verandahs;
Low-pitched hipped or
  gabled rooflines;
Unornamented surfaces;
Art-glass windows;
Asymmetrical floor plans.

Major Influences:
Japanese styles;
The Chicago School.

Where and When:
Chicago and the
  Midwest; c. 1905–30.

ABOVE: *The Robie House was constructed of brick and concrete, its horizontal planes and austere surfaces revealing little of its interior characteristics.*
BELOW: *Doorway detail of the Prairie style Woodbury County Courthouse, Sioux City, Iowa.*

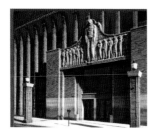

Distinguishing Characteristics

The distinctive Prairie house is easily recognized by the broad, horizontal planes, low-pitched rooflines, and large, cantilevered eaves and terraces that are common to almost all examples. The planes are always arranged at right angles and composed of woodwork or repeating courses of masonry, usually brick and concrete. The roofline may be broken by a rectangular central chimney. From the outside, little can be glimpsed of the interior because the outer boundaries are designed to create privacy and sheltered outdoor spaces that shield access to windows, entrances, and terraces. Inside, the spaces are light, open, and flowing, with few partitions to interrupt the sightlines through the carefully planned spaces.

BELOW: *An interior view of the Robie House's spacious, light living room, whose harmonious furnishings, art-glass windows, and decor were all custom-designed by Wright.*

Chicago-Area Examples

The William Winslow House (1893) in River Forest, Illinois, was a precursor of the Prairie style, with Chicago School features. The full-blown style took off quickly in the Chicago suburb of Oak Park, Wright's home during the formative part of his career. The area still boasts more than two dozen examples, including the 1901 stucco Frank W. Thomas House, and the Arthur Heurtley House, built in 1902 of brick. The magnificent Frederick C. Robie House in Chicago's Hyde Park is, however, considered the definitive example of the style.

The Prairie Style After Wright

Prairie-house designs were essentially simple and unpretentious and could be built inexpensively (though Wright himself spent lavishly on some of his Prairie homes). The open, functional designs were popularized beyond the Midwest by pattern books. Commercial and civic buildings followed, notably the Woodbury County Court-house in Sioux City, Iowa.

RUSTIC STYLES

Easily identifiable and now back in vogue, Rustic architecture is best exemplified by U.S. state- and national-park lodges, although it had its origins in the British Arts and Crafts movement, and is also frequently seen in residential buildings.

STYLE FILE

Notable Features:
Unpeeled-log framing;
Thatch or bark roofing;
Boulder walls and
 chimneys;
Informal design;
Corner notches with
 exposed log ends;
Steep rooflines;
Overhanging eaves;
Porches with railings of
 unpeeled timbers;
Large fireplaces (with
 stone-slab mantels)
 and chimneys.

Major Influences:
Arts and Crafts principles;
Log homes;
Local influences.

Where and When:
Worldwide, from late-19th
 century; "Parkitecture"
 in the United States,
 c. 1920–40.

Based on Nature

Drawing on the ideas of Arts and Crafts proponents like John Ruskin (*see* pages 192–93) and Gustav Stickley (*see* page 211), Andrew Jackson Downing, the earliest notable American landscape architect, first cultivated the Rustic style in its most coherent, recognizable form, as expressed in U.S. national-park lodges and cabins (a style that became known as "Parkitecture" or "Government Rustic"). Downing suggested that the structures best suited to landscape design were those that were based on nature—structures made of materials like unpeeled logs, thatch, bark, and stone "arranged in a natural manner."

Depression-Era Structures

Prominent Rustic-style structures were built in national parks including Yellowstone, Yosemite, and the Grand Canyon. During the Depression, President Franklin D. Roosevelt created the Civilian Conservation Corps (C.C.C.), in order

"to attack the enemies of erosion and deforestation" in America's parklands. C.C.C. workers built their own cabins in the parks for themselves and their families to live in—Rustic cabins that were clustered into groups or camps, with outdoor fireplaces and a larger log or stone building serving as the park headquarters and supply store. Several regional U.S. variants of Rustic styles were named for mountain ranges, including the influential Adirondack style.

ABOVE: *Ahwahnee Lodge, Yosemite, California.*

OPPOSITE: *The national-park lodge at Timberline, Oregon, an example of the Cascadian style.*

LEFT: *Rustic buildings are often just as rustic on the inside, with exposed timber or stone, or partition walls paneled with a local wood, and fireplaces built of irregularly placed stones.*

BUNGALOW

The word "bungalow" is derived from the Hindi *bangla*, which means "Bengali style," and the roots of this style stretch back to the Indian Subcontinent. Translated to a Western context, the bungalow is a single-story, detached dwelling with a low-pitched roof and verandah (*veranda* also being Hindi).

STYLE FILE

Notable Features:
A single-story, or one-and-a-half story, detached domestic dwelling set within its own small plot of land.
A low-pitched roof, sometimes providing attic space.
A verandah or porch, with square supports, either running the length of one wall or encircling the entire structure.
Timber-framed, with exposed wooden joints and rafters.
Wide eaves, often unenclosed and overhanging doors or windows.
Partly open-plan interiors.

Major Influences:
India's hill stations;
Prairie Style;
Craftsman homes;
The demand for inexpensive housing for middle-income families.

Where and When:
England and the United States; c.1870–1930.

From India to England

Upon their retirement, most British administrators of the Raj left India and returned to the United Kingdom, bringing with them a taste for the exotic-seeming hill-station houses, ventilated by their cooling verandahs. While the Indian "bungalow" could be multi-storied, in the West the bungalow was a relatively modest, single-story house. Nostalgia apart, their advantages included the ease and modest expense with which they could be erected, their practical design (particularly for older people with impaired mobility), and their limited maintenance requirements.

ABOVE, RIGHT: *A classic American bungalow (1916) of the broad-eaved California style, in Thompson Falls, Montana.*
RIGHT: *A modern "bungalow" in Bangalore, India.*

LEFT: *A typical British bungalow, brick-built with side gables (and second story added).*

BELOW: *An American Raised Ranch, an extremely popular two-story version of the flexible bungalow style.*

American Bungalow Style

The same considerations recommended bungalows to the United States, where, from around 1905, they were popularized by the Craftsman-style (*see* pages 210–11) designs of Californian architects Charles Sumner Greene (1868–1957) and Henry Mather Greene (1870–1954). Bungalow plans were soon made widely available through their publication in pattern books. Rather than serving as retirement houses, however, they made ideal homes for families of modest means. Although their ground plans and fundamental construction features remained essentially similar, the styling of American bungalows varied widely, with the Prairie, Craftsman, Ranch, Cape Cod, California, and American Foursquare styles being most prevalent, perhaps because, in an increasingly depersonalized, industrial age, they recalled the cozy simplicity and human values of rural living and the pioneer years.

THE CAPE COD COTTAGE

The Cape Cod cottage originated as a variant of the English Colonial house, with a single story. Its present-day incarnation took off in the 1930s: the classic Cape has an upper story with dormer windows and, usually, a porch projecting from the front facade.

CRAFTSMAN/MISSION

The Craftsman, or Mission, style was inspired by the British Arts and Crafts movement, but soon developed its own, American-specific aesthetic. Named after *The Craftsman,* the pioneering magazine launched by Gustav Stickley in 1901, this holistic style cherished Utopian aims for unpretentious lifestyles lived in utilitarian houses amid functional furnishings.

STYLE FILE

Notable Features:
A rustic appearance,
  with exposed structural
  components acting as
  decorative features;
A harmonious blending
  with the surroundings;
Natural, native materials;
Horizontal emphasis;
Asymmetrical massing;
Carefully designed
  interiors featuring
  handcrafted elements
  and furniture, including
  built-in features,
  fireplaces, and
  chimneys;
Casement windows,
  often with art glass.

Major Influences:
Mass production and
  industrialization;
The Arts and Crafts
  movement in Britain;
The Prairie style;
Local traditions and
  building materials.

Where and When:
The United States;
  c. 1900–30.

A Pan-American Mission

The principles that underpinned this style included the desire to return to traditional materials and ways of working, and an emphasis on the local, rather than the global, all manifested through honest, individualistic handicraft rather than the homogeneous, soulless mass production that was becoming ever more prevalent. The movement blossomed across the United States as the nineteenth century gave way to the twentieth, with Californian architects Greene & Greene popularizing Craftsman homes (sometimes known as "Ultimate Bungalows") on the West Coast; Frank Lloyd Wright and others founding the Chicago Arts and Crafts Society in 1897; and furniture maker Gustav Stickley and art-glass and interior designer Louis Comfort Tiffany (1848–1933) honing their uniquely American style on the East Coast.

OPPOSITE, ABOVE: *A Craftsman home in Darien, Connecticut.*
RIGHT AND OPPOSITE, BELOW: *The "ultimate bungalow"-style Gamble House, Pasadena, California (1909).*

Regional Variations

Because of the local emphasis, the Craftsman style varied from region to region, while still remaining true to its principles. Thus the Mission, Spanish, Pueblo, Log Cabin, and Cape Cod styles, as well as such period-revival styles as Tudor and colonial styles, can all be regarded as sheltering under the Craftsman umbrella. Although constructed on a far larger scale than most Craftsman homes, Charles Sumner Greene and Henry Mather Greene's Gamble House in Pasadena, California (1909), is regarded as being the showhouse of this style of architecture.

"TRUTH IN MATERIALS"

Gustav Stickley (1858–1942) was the leading light of the Craftsman movement. Having started out making chairs in his uncle's factory, he and his brothers established their New York–based company, Stickley Brothers, during the 1880s. From 1901 to 1916, *The Craftsman* brought his work and philosophy to a wider audience: it documented the construction and furnishing of firstly his home in Syracuse, and then his Craftsman Farms venture in Morris Plains, New Jersey. Stickley furniture was typically crafted from indigenous timber, simple and solid, yet functional and attractive, and, above all, quite timeless in its design.

ART NOUVEAU

Art Nouveau derives its name from La Maison de l'Art Nouveau ("The House of the New Art"), a store/gallery opened by Siegfried Bing in Paris, France, in 1895, to showcase the work of the craftsmen–artists who had initiated this style.

STYLE FILE

Notable Features:
Sinuous, undulating,
  organic forms;
Lavish, decorative
  ornamentation.

Major Influences:
Fluid plant forms and
  the natural world;
Stylized, linear, Japanese
  art;
The British Arts and
  Crafts movement.

Where and When:
Europe and the U.S.A.;
c.1890–1910.

RIGHT: *Victor Horta's Hotel Tassel (1893–94), Brussels, was the first Art Nouveau landmark.*
BELOW: *An Hector Guimard station entrance on the Paris Métro (subway).*

The Rejection of Conservatism

Art Nouveau's newness lay in its rejection of the rigidly formal, Classical idiom then held as the ideal by academies of fine arts in favor of a more flowing, expressive style. As well as being antihistorical, the proponents of Art Nouveau denounced the mass-produced uniformity of the Industrial Revolution era. Although they prized the spirit of individuality, their work had certain common links.

Horta Leads the Way

That Victor Horta (1861–1947) pioneered Art Nouveau architecture in 1892 is evident in the sinuous, iron tendrils with which he

ALTERNATIVE NAMES

The Art Nouveau style is known by a number of alternative names in Europe. For example, it is often called *Sezessionsstil* (see pages 214–15) in Austria; *Jugendstil* (see pages 214–15) in Germany; *stil floreale* ("floral style") or *stil Liberty* (after Liberty, the influential store in London, England) in Italy; and *arte noven* ("new art") or *Modernisme* (see pages 216–17) in Spain.

LEFT: *The entrance to a colliery in Dortmund, Germany,*

embellished his Hôtel Tassel in Brussels, Belgium, his Hôtel Solvay (1895–1900) and Maison du Peuple (1895–9), both also in Brussels, being equally innovative. Architects in other European cities seized the Art Nouveau baton, with Hector Guimard (1867–1942) being responsible for the eye-catching Castel Bérenger (1894–8), an apartment block, as well as the undulating cast-iron arches that he created between 1899 and 1904 to mark the entrances to Métro (subway) stations in Paris, France.

BELOW: *The Grand Hotel Evropa (Europa), 1903–6, designed by Bendelmayer and Drayek, in Prague.*

Art Nouveau Crosses the Atlantic
Art Nouveau found its expression in the United States, too, albeit in a distinctive new form, notably in the work of Louis Sullivan (*see* pages 200–1), whose steel-framed structures like Chicago's Carson, Pirie, Scott building bore Art Nouveau's imprint in the form of their decorative exterior ornamentation.

SECESSION/JUGENDSTIL

The Austrian interpretation of the principles underpinning Art Nouveau was termed *Sezessionsstil* ("Secession style"), underlining the significance of the Wiener (Vienna) Sezession's break with the past, while the German name *Jugendstil* ("youth style") reflects the invigorating impact of the new style.

STYLE FILE

Notable Features:
The combination of a rectilinear form with curvilinear, decorative ornamentation;
The restrained use of Classical motifs;
White-marble "backdrops."

Major Influences:
Linear Japanese art forms;
The British architect Charles Voysey (1857–1941);
Charles Rennie Mackintosh and the Glasgow School;
Art Nouveau;
The Austrian painters Gustav Klimt (1862–1918) and Koloman Moser (1868–1918).

Where and When:
Austria (particularly Vienna), c. 1898–1911, and Germany, c. 1896–1910.

The Secession's Viennese Showcase

When the Austrian architects Josef Maria Olbrich (1867–1908) and Josef Hoffmann (1870–1956) joined such artists as Gustav Klimt in breaking free of the Classical strictures of Vienna's Academy of Fine Arts and setting up the Vienna Secession in 1897, they faced the problem of where to base themselves. Olbrich's monumental Secession Building (1898), with its striking, apical dome constructed of perforated metal, provided a solution, as well as a bold statement of intent. Another significant Viennese Secession construction is the Post Office Savings Bank that was completed by Otto Wagner (1841–1918) in 1904, a white-marble-faced building that utilizes aluminum as a decorative material.

RIGHT: *The golden dome atop Joseph Maria Olbrich's 1897 Secession Building in Vienna, Austria. The inscription reads: "To every age its art and to art its freedom." The building is ornamented with "eel" or "whiplash" stylized figures.*

INTEGRATING THE APPLIED ARTS

The leading lights of the *Sezessionsstil* and *Jugendstil* aimed to create a seamless fusion between art, design, and craft, and to this end created a number of influential associations. They included the Deutsche Werkstätten ("German Workshops," established in Dresden, Germany, in 1898), the Wiener Werkstätte ("Vienna Workshops," Vienna, Austria, 1903), and the Deutscher Werkbund ("German Work Federation," Munich, Germany, 1907).

ABOVE: *The Secession style was popular across central Europe. This is one of several notable Secessionist buildings in Oradea, Romania.*

BELOW: *The Topic Building (1906), by Osvald Polívka, in Prague, the Czech Republic.*

Sezessionsstil Branches Out

In 1899, Olbrich moved to Darmstadt, Germany, to help to establish an artists' colony. Here, he contributed to the Mathildenhöhe, a complex that included his Ernst Ludwig House (1901), the Exhibition Hall (1908), and the Hochzeitsturm (or "Wedding Tower," also 1908). And one of Hoffmann's most acclaimed buildings was the Palais Stoclet ("Stoclet Palace") (1905–10) in Brussels, Belgium, with its rectangular, white-marble-fronted, structural components and decorative, articulated-metal banding and gilded friezes.

Germany's *Jugendstil*

The name *Jugendstil* is derived from *Die Jugend* ("*Youth*"), an avant-garde periodical that was first published in Munich in 1896. Noteworthy *Jugendstil* architects include Hermann Obrist (1863–1927) and August Endell (1871–1925).

CATALAN MODERNISM

In Spain, Art Nouveau (*arte noven* in Spanish, *see* pages 212–13), which was also termed *Modernisme*—"Modernism"—found its most remarkable expression in the Catalonian city of Barcelona, and particularly in the extraordinary creations of Antoni Gaudí (1852–1926).

STYLE FILE

Notable Features:
Brick-built structures;
Fluid, curvilinear, organic forms;
An exuberant mixture of decorative ornamentation;
Eccentric individualism.

Major Influences:
Catalan nationalism;
Gothic architecture;
Moorish, Moroccan, and Islamic architecture;
Art Nouveau.

Where and When:
The Catalonian region of northern Spain, specifically Barcelona; c.1880–1920.

OPPOSITE, ABOVE: *The distinctive spires of the Sagrada Família, an iconic structure that is Barcelona's best-known landmark.*

OPPOSITE, BELOW: *The colorful Parc Güell, Barcelona; one of the entrance buildings is visible behind a terrace wall.*

RIGHT: *The Casa Milá, Barcelona, by Gaudí: detail of the roof, chimneys, and ventilation shafts.*

Expressing the Catalan Spirit

Lluis Domènech i Montaner (1849–1923) is credited with initiating Catalonia's late-nineteenth-century architectural flowering in the form of an article entitled "*En busca de una arquitectura nacional*" ("In search of a national architecture"), in the periodical *La Renaixença* ("*The Renaissance*"), in 1878. His own contributions to developing the new Catalan style included Barcelona's Palau de la Música Catalana ("Palace of Catalan Music," 1904–8), a concert hall covered with decorative sculptures, reliefs, and mosaics. Among the other architects who enthusiastically embraced the creative challenge of expressing Catalonia's national spirit through architecture were Josep Puig i Cadafalch (1869–1956), the horizontality of whose brick Barcelonan Casaramona Factory (1912) is broken up by Gothic-style parapets and two soaring water towers.

LA SAGRADA FAMÍLIA

Antoni Gaudí worked on this Roman Catholic basilica for more than forty years, entirely devoting the last fifteen years of his life to it. His vision for the building incorporated much mystic symbolism: on completion, eighteen tall towers will represent, in ascending order of height, the twelve Apostles, the four Evangelists, the Virgin Mary, and Jesus Christ. The Evangelists' towers will be topped with sculptures of their traditional symbols—a bull, angel, eagle, and lion. The magnificent doors of the Passion facade, completed in 1987, are inscribed with words from the Bible in various languages. Areas of the sanctuary will represent themes like saints, virtues, and sins. At the latest estimate, it is expected to be completed in 2026, the 100th anniversary of Gaudí's death.

The Great Gaudí

Barcelona is filled with gems of Catalan Modernism, the most glittering being those crafted by Gaudí. Sagrada Família ("Holy Family") remains a work in progress, as it was when Gaudí was commissioned to continue developing what was then a nascent neo-Gothic church in 1883, whose spires he subsequently transformed into structures resembling termite hills. Such buildings as the Palacio Güell (1885–89) and the Casa Milá (1910) are topped with equally organic-looking roof projections, while many of Gaudí's constructions are decorated with his hallmark undulating facades, wrought-iron balconies, and brightly colored, ceramic mosaics.

CONSTRUCTIVISM

Although the Russian artist Vladimir Tatlin (1885–1953) is credited with founding Constructivism in 1913, it was not until 1921, when the First Working Group of Constructivists convened in Moscow, that the Constructivists issued a manifesto.

STYLE FILE

Public, rather than
  domestic, buildings;
An emphasis on struc-
  ture and utilitarianism
  rather than referential
  decoration;
Abstract, nonrepresenta-
  tional, geometric forms.

Major Influences:
Cubism, Suprematism,
  Futurism, Neo-
  Plasticism, the
  Bauhaus;
Industrial technology
  and the machine: its
  structure, components,
  and function;
The physical properties
  inherent in specific
  materials;
Communist ideology.

Where and When:
The Soviet Union (partic-
  ularly Russia and the
  Ukraine); c. 1913–30.

Radical Architecture for a Revolutionary Society

By 1921, it had been four years since the Bolshevik revolutionaries overthrew Russia's feudal, Czarist order and replaced it with an egalitarian, Communist regime, in the process creating an increasingly industrialized society in which the machines that so inspired the Constructivists played a vital part.

Indeed, the Constructivist celebration of the integrity of such materials as concrete and steel, combined with their preference for simple, geometric forms, seemed perfectly ideologically suited to the "pure" new social and political order, which may be why most Constructivist architecture took the form of public, not private, buildings.

OPPOSITE: *A 1930s' Constructivist building in Ekaterinburg, Russia, now converted to a hotel.*

RIGHT: *Constructivist buildings on Ekaterinburg's Lenin Prospekt.*

Experimental Visionaries

Tatlin's best-known contribution to the Constructivist canon was doomed to remain unconstructed, namely his Monument to the Third International (1920, *see* feature). Many more proposed structures in this experimental style similarly became victims of a combination of national economic difficulty and prohibitive construction costs, including the Lenin Institute (1927), by Ivan Leonidov (1902–59), whose design focused on a glass rectangle and sphere suspended above the ground, the complex being accessed from nearby Moscow by monorail. Other blueprints were realized, however, among them such "social condensers" as Moscow's concrete Rusakov Club (1927–28), by Konstantin Melnikov (1890–1974), which is remarkable for the blocklike sections of auditorium that project from the body of the building like crenelations turned on their side.

MONUMENT TO THE THIRD INTERNATIONAL

Vladimir Tatlin designed this 1920 model of a proposed Eiffel Tower–sized, spiraling symbol of Soviet engineering prowess and modernity. However, despite being widely celebrated, "Tatlin's Tower" was never built at full size.

ART DECO: THE JAZZ AGE

Art Deco, the style that rose to prominence during the Jazz Age and was cur-
tailed by the outbreak of World War II, derives its name from the Exposition
Internationale des Arts Décoratifs et Industriels Modernes (International Exposition of Modern Decorative and Industrial Arts) held in Paris, France, in 1925.

The Jazz Age Style

The bold, futuristic vision and elegant,
streamlined shapes of 1920s' Art Deco architecture perfectly symbolize the zeitgeist of
the post–World War I Jazz Age, and specifically the emphatic desire to reject the blood-
shed, misery, and deprivation of the recent
past in favor of building a brave new world in
which democracy, clinical efficiency, capitalism, and even luxury prevailed. But if the past
were to be referenced, it would be the ancient
past, and the motifs and symbols of such early
civilizations as pharaonic Egypt that would be
subjected to a stylized, twentieth-century
reinterpretation (prompted in part by the dis-
covery of King Tutankhamen's tomb in 1922).
Thus, for example, the pyramidal form of
New York's Barclay-Vesey Building (1923), by

LEFT: *The world-famous Empire State Building, New York City. More than 1,800 stairs extend from the lobby to the 102nd floor.*

OPPOSITE: *The Los Angeles Public Library (1926) was designed by Bertram Goodhue. Its tower is capped by a pyramid that refers to ancient Egypt's library at Alexandria.*

THE EMPIRE STATE BUILDING

Location: 350 Fifth Avenue, New York City.
Completed: 1931.
Architect: William Lamb, of Shreve, Lamb, and Harmon Associates.
Height: 1,454 feet (on its completion, it was the world's tallest skyscraper).
Number of Stories: 102.
Exterior Materials: Indiana limestone and marble.
Notable Features: The Observatory, an observation deck on the 86th floor, is one of two viewing platforms from which more than 100 million visitors have admired New York. The floodlights are lit nightly, illuminating the upper stories; colored lights are used for special occasions. Originally planned as a mooring mast for zeppelins, the antenna also functions as a lightning conductor.

Ralph Walker (1889–1973) for McKenzie, Voorhees, and Gmelin, can be said to resemble a Mayan stepped temple or Babylonian ziggurat. And although it was in France that the purest form of Art Deco originated—expressed, for example, by Robert Mallet-Stevens (1886–1945) in his residential complex (1926–27) in the rue Mallet-Stevens, Auteuil, Paris—and from which it was disseminated, it found its brashest, most breathtaking expression in a richer, more confident, and younger nation, namely the United States.

ART DECO: STREAMLINE

As the Art Deco style matured, the use of stylized, historical motifs as ornamentation gradually gave way to simpler, geometric devices (like the Chrysler Building's chevrons), and, eventually, to a sleeker, plainer, "streamlined" look.

STYLE FILE

Notable Features:
Simple, streamlined, geometric forms, emphasis becoming curvilinear;
Stylized decorative motifs, but gradually becoming plainer than early Art Deco buildings;
Curved, wraparound corner windows.

Major Influences:
Early Art Deco;
Ocean liners;
Modernist ideas of purity of form.

Where and When:
The United States, spreading to Western Europe; 1930s.

RIGHT: *The Cincinnati Museum Center was originally built as the city's Union Terminal, 1929–33, and designed by French-American architect Paul-Philippe Cret.*

OPPOSITE: *Two detail views in Miami Beach, Florida, a city that boasts its own Art Deco style. This is called "MiMo" (a contraction of "Miami Moderne"), "Streamline Moderne," or "Art Moderne" (not to be confused with the International style, with which it overlaps: see pages 230–31).*

The Big Apple's Skyscrapers

While the cutting-edge architects of Western Europe experimented with various avant-garde styles, it was the United States, and particularly such centers of wealth as New York, that led the way in the development of rectilinear Art Deco structures, whose most striking form was the skyscraper. Perhaps the most famous skyscrapers from this era are New York City's iconic Chrysler Building (1928–30), by William Van Alen (1882–1954), with its tapering, four-sided dome featuring a repeated sunburst motif that was modeled on the radiator cap of the 1929 Chrysler car, and the Empire State Building (1931, *see* page 221), which was designed by the architectural firm of Shreve, Lamb, and Harmon Associates. Raymond Hood (1881–1934) was arguably the most accomplished Art Deco architect working in New York, however, being especially acclaimed for the towering R.C.A. Building (1933, now 30 Rockefeller Plaza), in the Rockefeller Center.

Curves, Sleek Lines, and Moderne

The onset of the Depression at the start of the 1930s heralded the scaling-down of the skyscraper and the advent of a more curvilinear form of Art Deco, a style that lent itself to railroad stations and domestic buildings. Havana, Cuba, and Miami, Florida, boast many Art Deco architectural jewels, including, in Miami, the Essex House (1938), by Henry Hohauser (1895–1963), a prolific architect working in Miami Beach and master of the "Nautical Moderne" style, whose curved, wraparound corner windows are flanked by trios of porthole windows, giving the structure an appropriately linerlike appearance in view of its seaside location.

CHRYSLER BUILDING

Location: 405 Lexington Avenue, New York City.
Completed: 1930.
Architect: W. Van Alen.

Height: 1,048 feet (to the top of the spire).
Number of Stories: 77.
Exterior Materials: Stainless steel.
Notable Features: The radiator-cap gargoyles, sunburst motif, and tiered spire are among its best-loved exterior features. The lobby is of pink African marble.

FUNCTIONALISM

The Functionalist movement in architecture began in earnest with the dictum "Form ever follows function," coined by Louis Sullivan (*see* pages 200–1), and taken on board by Frank Lloyd Wright and many others—but it probably originated long before. Under Functionalist principles, the architect's primary consideration is the end use of the building; its aesthetics flow from there.

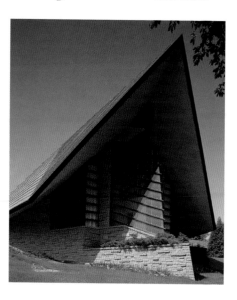

STYLE FILE

Notable Features:
Shape is dictated by the use of the building and/or needs of its intended occupants; Ornamentation is usually minimal, restrained or entirely absent;

Major Influences:
A.W.N. Pugin;
Louis Sullivan;
Frank Lloyd Wright.

Where and When:
North America, Australia, Europe, and eventually, worldwide, from the early 20th century to the present day.

ABOVE: *Frank Lloyd Wright's Unitarian Meeting House, Sherwood Hills, Wisconsin. Light from the glass wall fills the sanctuary from behind the pulpit.*

OPPOSITE, BELOW: *Hans Scharoun's Berlin Philharmonic building was designed "from the inside, out."*

What's the Use?

While it may seem obvious that an architect's job is to consider the use of a building, it is not a given that form should follow function. If one considers, for example, Rococo buildings (*see* pages 92–93), much of the design work has been devoted to the ornamentation, which itself has little or nothing to do with its use. By contrast, in Frank Lloyd Wright's Unitarian Meeting House (1946, Wisconsin), the building's form is itself an expression of reverence, pointing heavenward, replacing the traditional steeple and symbolizing worship. Wright created beautiful, functional spaces for congregations of various faiths.

Sound and Vision

German architect Hugo Häring was influential in social housing projects of the 1920s and '30s, arguing that the site and client's needs should dictate form. Working with fellow German Hans Scharoun, he designed housing at Siemensstadt, a project in Berlin, focusing on social space and with landscaped outdoor areas. In his design for the Berlin Philharmonic (1965–63), Scharoun made acoustics the starting point, allowing the shape of the building to be formed around a central stage, with surrounding audience seating and a layered ceiling.

NEW OBJECTIVITY

German architects of the 1920s and '30s embraced a *Neue Sachlichkeit*, or New Objectivity, in rejecting sentimental architecture and concentrating on function. Erich Mendelsohn and Bruno Taut were among those who combined elements of De Stijl's and Frank Lloyd Wright's design principles and applied them to social housing. Frankfurt-am-Main has good examples of social housing built in this style and under the New Objectivity ethic.

ABOVE: *One of Hugo Häring's Functional apartment blocks at Siemensstadt (1929–31), Berlin. It features balconies acting as an extra room for most of the units, and communal spaces.*

USONIAN

Just as the English humanist Thomas More conceived of an idealized place called Utopia, so Frank Lloyd Wright's American dream, first outlined in 1928, focused on "U.S.-onia," where the uniquely American state of mind and experience would find authentic, egalitarian expression in the built environment.

OPPOSITE: *The Zimmerman House (1950), Manchester, New Hampshire.*

RIGHT: *The Jacobs House (1936), Madison, Wisconsin: the first Usonian house. The square-shaped units on which the modular grid is based are visible in the floor surface.*

All-American Dream Homes

To this end, and also influenced by the economic depression that prevailed during the 1930s, Wright was inspired to democratize his designs for domestic dwellings to make them available to ordinary Americans. This meant ensuring that their construction costs were low, which he achieved by simplification and mass production, while never compromising the quality or humanity of his designs. Thus Wright ensured that Usonian homes were warm by incorporating radiant-heating elements in their foundation, yet still made the hearth a focal point, and generally ensured that low construction and maintenance costs were not achieved at the expense of space, comfort, or convenience. It was also a vital

part of Wright's concept that the interior, exterior, and surroundings of his Usonian houses should harmonize with one another, regardless of where they were built.

Usonia Across the United States

The first Usonian home was the L-shaped Jacobs House (1936), Madison, Wisconsin, with later acclaimed examples following over the next two decades, such as the Greg Affleck House (1941), Bloomfield Hills, Michigan, and the Toufic L. Kalil House (1955), Manchester, New Hampshire. During the 1950s, Wright coined the term "Usonian Automatic" for what were literally home-assembly, modular, concrete-block kit houses that aspiring homeowners could (at least, in theory) construct themselves, a prime example of these being the Gerald B. Tonkens House (1954), Amberly Village, Ohio.

INTERIOR SPACE

True to his "destruction of the box" ethos, Wright did away with many of the dividing walls that demarcated communal spaces in more traditional homes. "We can never make the living room big enough, the fireplace important enough, or the sense of relationship between exterior, interior, and environment close enough, or get enough of these good things I've just mentioned. A Usonian house is always hungry for the ground, lives by it, becoming an integral feature of it." (quoted in *The Architectural Forum*, January 1948.)

BAUHAUS

Bauhaus (from the German *bauen*, "to build," and *Haus*, "house") was not just an architectural and design movement, but a Utopian vision of a new world of functional, efficient construction for a new generation in the machine age.

STYLE FILE

Notable Features:
Clean, plain lines;
Functional design;
Flat roofs (usually);
Minimal ornamentation,
  featuring smooth sur-
  faces of white or gray;
Horizontal window strips;
Open-plan, light interiors
  with built-in fixtures;
Reinforced concrete;
Some buildings con-
  structed on "stilts."

Major Influences:
Frank Lloyd Wright;
The Arts and Crafts
  movement.

Where and When:
Germany and Tel Aviv;
1919–33 (1930s in Israel).

The Bauhaus Vision

The movement began in Weimar, Germany, in 1919, when Walter Gropius became director of the Bauhaus school of design (which was later moved to Dessau). In his manifesto outlining the school's aims, he stated that "The ultimate aim of all creative activity is a building. ... Architects, painters, and sculptors must again get to know and comprehend the composite character of a building, both as an entity and in terms of its various parts." For Gropius and his colleagues, notably Mies van der Rohe and Le Corbusier, "There is no essential difference between the artist and the craftsman." Their ideal was to create "rational" social housing for modern workers, who would live in a well-designed, attractive, planned environment that they would value, and thus take pride in, resulting in a better standard of living for all.

A Minimalist Aesthetic

Bauhaus buildings were functional, smooth, efficient, minimally adorned, light, open-plan, and affordable, with a unifying design tying in the building's exterior with its interior fixtures, fittings, and furnishings. The excessive ornamentation of the Victorian era was dismissed as decadent and superfluous. Like Frank Lloyd Wright, Gropius wanted all the details, from door handles and light fittings to furniture, to be designed specifically for a building (indeed, residents sometimes complained that their homes were overplanned, and thus somewhat impersonal). A team of artists, including Wassily Kandinsky and Paul Klee, helped provide creative inspiration as teachers at the school.

Gropius's design school has been called the most influential of the twentieth century. The Nazis, however, distrusted and detested the movement, deeming its design "rubbish" and out of step with "pure" German art: they closed the school in 1933, and the major figures left the country, mostly for the United States.

ABOVE: *The Walter Gropius House, Massachusetts.*
OPPOSITE: *The Bauhaus-Archiv design museum in Berlin is housed in a building designed by Gropius (built 1976–78).*

BAUHAUS CITY

While buildings in this style outside Germany are usually labeled "International style," the biggest concentration of Bauhaus architecture anywhere is in Israel's Tel Aviv, largely due to the building boom of the early 1930s and the influence of incoming Bauhaus graduates like Erich Mendelsohn. Today, the Bauhaus-dominated area of this so-called "White City" is a UNESCO World Heritage Site.

INTERNATIONAL STYLE

The International style (sometimes called Art Moderne) was rooted in the early years of the twentieth century, and particularly in the work of German architect Peter Behrens (1868–1940), designer of the A.E.G. Turbine Factory, Berlin (1908–9), and employer, in around 1910, of a trio of future stars.

STYLE FILE

Notable Features:
Cubic, rectilinear forms;
Horizontal orientations
  and low elevations;
Flat roofs;
Glass, steel, aluminum,
  and concrete;
White-painted walls;
Long, horizontal, metal-
  framed windows;
Absence of ornamentation;
Open-plan interiors.

Major Influences:
Peter Behrens;
Frank Lloyd Wright;
The De Stijl movement;
Functionalism;
Industrialization and
  technology;
Internationalism.

Where and When:
Western Europe, North
  America; c. 1925–45.

Behrens's Star Pupils

Architects who learned the importance of good, functional design from Peter Behrens included Walter Gropius (1883–1969) and Ludwig Mies van der Rohe (1886–1969)—two Germans—and Charles-Édouard Jeanneret, or "Le Corbusier" (1887–1966), who was Swiss. It was Gropius who, with Adolph Meyer (1881–1929), was responsible for arguably the first structure of the new style, the cubic, concrete, and glass Fagus Factory in Alfeld (1911), as well as the Bauhaus Building in Dessau (1925–26, *see* page 228), following his appointment to the directorship of the school of the same name (a position that Mies van der Rohe subsequently also held). Of the three, Le Corbusier is considered to have been the most influential, his buildings, such as the Villa Savoye, Poissy-sur-Seine, France (1929–31), having a strikingly austere purity of form.

LEFT: *The Lovell Beach House (1926), Newport Beach, California, by Rudolph M. Schindler.*

OPPOSITE: *Units at Aluminum City Terrace, New Kensington, Pennsylvania, designed by Gropius and Breuer (see feature, below).*

American Flourishing

Both Gropius and Mies van der Rohe propagated the seeds of the International style in the United States, to which they emigrated following the Nazi rise to power in Germany in 1933. Having become professor of architecture at the Illinois Institute of Technology in Chicago in 1938, Mies van der Rohe remained fundamentally true to this minimal, streamlined style from 1939, when he created a cubic campus at Chicago, until his death thirty years later, as did Gropius, who died in the same year, having instructed generations of students at Harvard University. (*See* pages 236–37 for later International Style works.)

The Name Game

The name "Art Moderne" is derived from the Congrès Internationaux d'Architecture Moderne, first convened in Switzerland in 1928. The term "International Style" was coined by the American architects Philip Johnson and Henry-Russell Hitchcock in 1932, for an exhibition held at New York's Museum of Modern Art. These terms are often considered synonymous, but "Art Moderne" is also used interchangeably with "Streamline," or "Streamline Moderne," in Florida (*see* pages 222–23).

INSET, BELOW: *An interior view of a single-story unit at Aluminum City Terrace.*

ALUMINUM CITY TERRACE

In 1941 Walter Gropius and Marcel Breuer were commissioned to design a government housing development in New Kensington, near Pittsburgh, Pennsylvania. Called Aluminum City Terrace, the community had 250 residential units in mixed-size multiunit structures, modern in style and with up-to-date gadgets and kitchen facilities. The housing proved popular and became a co-op in 1948.

ORGANIC (WRIGHT)

Despite spending his early years as an architect in Chicago, Frank Lloyd Wright disliked urban environments and instead found inspiration in nature. Thus he became a pioneer of "organic" architecture—a description that he coined in 1908—in which natural forms were translated into architectural shapes.

STYLE FILE

Notable Features:
Nature-inspired forms;
Functional design that is
built for occupants'
comfort and needs;
Buildings that appear to
have grown from their
natural surroundings;
Use of natural light;
Open-plan interiors;
Energy efficiency;
"Total design," in which
Interiors, ornament and
fittings harmonize with
exterior and setting;

Major Influences:
The natural world;
The "form follows
function" philosophy of
Louis Sullivan and
others.

Where and When:
The United States;
c. 1893–1959.

At One with Nature

Wright's innovative, "organic" approach was exemplified by the seashell-like Solomon R. Guggenheim Museum (1943–59) that he designed in New York. He furthermore believed that manmade constructions should meld so seamlessly with their natural environments that it were as if they had sprung up spontaneously, and had then evolved organically, reacting to, as well as interacting with, their surroundings almost as though they were living beings. Take Fallingwater (1936), at Mill Run, Pennsylvania, for example, below which the cascading stream that gives the house its name surges, whose cantilevered balconies and terraces echo the form of the rocky hillside from which they appear to have sprouted, and whose hearth was constructed around onsite boulders. Similarly, local desert rocks are embedded in the exterior and interior masonry at Taliesin West (1937–59), in Scottsdale, Arizona, Wright's home, architectural school, and work in progress.

OPPOSITE: *Fallingwater (1936),*
Wright's most famous work of
residential architecture.

RIGHT: *Exterior detail of*
Taliesin West, Wright's organic-
style home in the desert land-
scape of Scottsdale, Arizona.

Essential Engineering

Crucial to Wright's organic architecture were the sophisticated engineering techniques that underpinned his buildings, notably cantilevers and such ingenious supports as the dendriform (tree-shaped) concrete, steel-reinforced, mushroom columns supporting the glass roof of the S. C. Johnson & Son Administration Building (1936) in Racine, Wisconsin. Wright was bold in embracing new technology and ideas. Nor was he afraid of combining manmade and natural materials, so that while Fallingwater's vertical elements are of limestone, concrete was used to create its horizontal components.

POSTWAR MODERN ARCHITECTURE

The devastation and mass migrations of World War II and its aftermath would, inevitably, lead some architects to reject the past, preferring instead to look toward a brighter future. Others, though, chose to look to the past for reminders of what had been lost. Some decades later, a new generation of designers took inspiration from a more distant past—prehistory—or local folkways, seeking indigenous materials and methods in hopes of finding sustainable ways to build for a resource-scarce future.

Rather than following a linear path, the development of architecture since the mid-twentieth century has been characterized by a number of contradictions like this one. While some architects obscured any hint of a building's structure beneath enigmatic, reflective surfaces, others expressed structure more overtly than ever—celebrated it, even. Destroying the "box" and dissolving the geometry of architecture, Deconstructivists and "Blobitects" reinvented buildings, creating hitherto impossible forms, for example, while others emphasized the right angle and abstract, geometric patterns. And while some worked on the huge scale of a "total environment" or a superscraper, others exhorted us to believe that "small is beautiful."

OPPOSITE: *Detail of titanium cladding on the extension to the Denver Art Museum (the Frederic C. Hamilton Building), Colorado, opened 2006. Designed by Daniel Libeskind, its shape was inspired by the Rockies.*

POSTWAR INTERNATIONAL STYLE

In the years following World War II, International-style architects (*see* pages 230–31) responded to its horrors and destruction by focusing on unity, monumentality, and the power of technology. In a unanimous effort to ensure that these catastrophic events would never recur, the United Nations was founded, its New York headquarters designed by leading Internationalist architects.

THE UNITED NATIONS

Based on a design by Le Corbusier, a team of ten architects (including Wallace K. Harrison, Oscar Niemeyer, and Howard Robertson) created this potent postwar symbol. A majestic and sweeping structure of reinforced concrete, it also boasts New York City's first glass curtain wall and aluminum exterior.

Mies van der Rohe

Ludwig Mies van der Rohe, with his aesthetics of "architectural integrity" and "structural honesty," created large-scale, ascendant steel structures enrobed in glass curtain-wall facades. These buildings are bold and austere, but also exhibit his strong sense of proportion and attention to detail. His Seagrams Building, New York (1956–58, with Philip Johnson), exemplifies his famous "Less is more" maxim. Mies and the architects of the 1950s used the most modern materials and techniques available and fervently believed in the strength of technological progress and the future. As the leading architect of the International movement, his influence is seen in steel-and-glass office buildings throughout the world.

RIGHT: *Facade detail of the National Gallery of Canada (1986–88), Ottawa, designed by Moshe Safdie, who was influenced by the work of Philip Johnson.*

Bottles in a Wine Rack

The problem of housing shortages also needed to be addressed after the war. The first postwar building that Le Corbusier (Charles-Edouard Jeanneret) designed was the Unité d'Habitation in Marseilles, France, a utopian design for city dwelling. It is a concrete, rectilinear grid, raised on sculpted legs, into which prefabricated apartments were fitted like "bottles into a wine rack." It included stores, communal recreational spaces, and large balconies, which dominate the facade. Similar apartment complexes were repeated in cities throughout Europe.

The Marshall Plan

As victors of the war, Americans—and especially transplanted Europeans—dominated the architectural field, both at home and in the countries of Europe and Asia where the United States exerted its influence. Through initiatives like the Marshall Plan, America attempted to instill the ideology of capitalism and liberal democracy wherever she could. This included exchange programs between architects and engineers and proved influential throughout Europe and Asia.

ABOVE: *The Farnsworth House, designed by Mies van der Rohe, in Plano, Illinois (1946–51).*

SAMBA SAMBA

After Le Corbusier collaborated with Lucio Costa in 1936 on Rio de Janeiro's magnificent and influential Ministry of Education and Health, Brazil adopted the International style. In 1957 Costa's designs were chosen for Brazil's ambitious plans for a new capital at Brasilia. Oscar Niemeyer was a young architect in Costa's office who worked on the Ministry of Education and Health. He went on to design many of the buildings in the new capital, including the cathedral, and is widely considered to be Le Corbusier's tropical successor, but with an emphasis on free form.

WRIGHT: MATURE PERIOD

Frank Lloyd Wright's most prolific phase spanned the period from the 1940s to his death in 1959. During this time he designed almost five hundred projects, representing approximately half of the output of his entire career.

A SPIRAL PROCESS

Despite Guggenheim's enthusiasm for the spiral museum design, after his death in 1949, the museum's board was less approving. Before ground was broken in 1956, more land had been acquired and the plans had been redesigned no less than seven times. The building was finally ready six months after Wright's death in 1959.

BELOW: *The organic, concrete Kalita Humphreys Theater, Dallas (1955), has been called "the Guggenheim of the West."*

Ramping It Up

Wright's most famous, and possibly most controversial, building of this period is the Solomon R. Guggenheim Museum in New York City (1943–59). Because of the narrow site, the design had to be vertical, and from the first, Wright envisaged the now-iconic ramp that is continuous throughout the building, encircling the central interior column. The resulting curved form of molded concrete reinforced by steel remains one of the city's most recognizable landmarks. Visitors appreciate the slightly angled walls that give paintings the appearance of being seen on an easel and the galleries that gently evolve from one story to another. However, critics of the building claim that the interior doesn't work and that it was "Wright's revenge," as he did not care for New York City, or for museums.

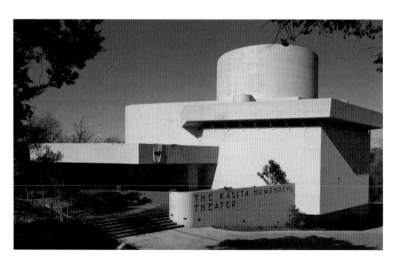

Pride of Marin County

One of Wright's final projects was his only government commission, the Marin County Civic Center in San Rafael, California (1957). The center was to house thirteen county departments and to comprise an administration and hall of justice building, and there were preliminary plans for a theater, auditorium, fairground pavilion, and lagoon. The central features are a massive flattened dome juxtaposed with a tower and the long, thin rectangle of the administration and hall of justice building. The result is the perfect culmination of his canon, architecture infused with emotion, informed by, and informing, its landscape.

ABOVE: *The soaring tower of the Marin County Civic Center.* RIGHT: *The pyramidal Beth Shalom Synagogue, Elkins Park, Pennsylvania (1954).*

THE HILLS OF MARIN

The site chosen for the Marin County Civic Center was spread over three hills, which the commissioning board anticipated would have to be removed. Wright, as was his custom, instead allowed himself to be inspired by the landscape. He embraced the challenge of the setting and the complex nature of the multiuse buildings and created a bold, modern, futuristic design for the hilly site. The buildings have contrasting forms to distinguish the different internal functions.

MODERNISM

Modernism has become the world's most prolific building style. Evolving from the utilitarian forms introduced in the nineteenth century, the aesthetic adopted principles of the International style, but was freer in its geometric forms.

STYLE FILE

Notable Features:
Simple, clean lines;
Cylinders and unusually
  shaped buildings;
Slanted or curved roofs;
Unadorned facades.

Major Influences:
Rejection of historicism;
Early Modern styles,
  especially the
  International style.

Where and When:
Worldwide; 1940s
  onward.

Shapes and Sizes

Starting in the 1960s, Modernist design became more creative in the variety of shapes and structures that it encompassed. This style is marked by cylindrical buildings, sloped roofs, and unusual shapes. Modernism was a trend that prevailed despite the emergence of Postmodernism, due to the appeal, both economically and aesthetically, of its inherent simplicity. Stubbins Associates, Inc., is a firm that has produced some of the most recognizable examples of the style, as well as the tallest building in Japan (the Yokohama Landmark Tower, 1993).

OPPOSITE: *The Pacific Design Center (nicknamed the "Blue Whale"), Los Angeles, California, designed by Cesar Pelli, 1975, was clearly influenced by the simple forms of Modernism.*

RIGHT: *Congress Hall (1956–57), in the Tiergarten, Berlin, Germany, designed by Hugh Stubbins with Werner Düttmann and Franz Mocken. The building is informally known as the "Pregnant Oyster."*

Visual Drama

One of the most dynamic Modernist additions to the New York skyline came in 1977, with the completion of Citigroup Center. Its dramatically slanted roof was originally intended to hold solar panels. The building's drama is further enhanced by its base, which is cut away at all four corners, leaving it apparently perched on a cross-shaped footing. This feature was not a part of the original design, but was adopted to accommodate St. Peter's Lutheran Church when church leaders refused to give up their lot. Despite the employment of a computer-driven load-mass damper that ensures the stability of the building and permits fewer vertical supports, there were fears that the tower would collapse in high winds. At one point, with the threat of an approaching storm, crews worked around the clock to shore up the building.

CESAR PELLI

Cesar Pelli (b. Argentina, 1926) has won numerous awards, including, in 1995, the AIA Gold Medal, and has been listed as one of the ten most influential living American architects. Perhaps best known today for his Petronas Towers, Malaysia, his architecture places primary importance on simple, geometric forms and a building's exterior enclosure, or "skin," (often with glass being the material of choice), citing this as the element through which a building is located in the stream of architectural and construction history.

BRUTALISM

A pronounced, and much reviled, offshoot of the Modernist style (*see* pages 240–41) was Brutalism, whose buildings are similar in many respects to Modernist structures, but celebrate the rough qualities of concrete.

The Joy of Concrete

The style's name is derived from the French term *beton brut* ("rough concrete"), but there is an element of brutality as well in the stolid and unrefined molded surfaces that are generally made of exposed concrete. These buildings explore the simplicity of concrete in their crude, natural forms. Brick and glass were occasionally used, but again, the buildings conformed to the blocklike figures of the basic, blank-looking shapes of Brutalism.

OPPOSITE: *The Brutalists encouraged the trend for high-rise, apartment living.*
RIGHT AND BELOW: *Concrete and glass soon became standard materials for office buildings, parking lots, housing, and public buildings alike.*

Gray Matter

Interestingly, Le Corbusier is considered the founder of this style because of his experimentation with concrete and his designs for enormous block housing, but it was John Portman & Associates that popularized Brutalism with such buildings as Atlanta, Georgia's, Marriott Marquis Hotel (1985) and Singapore's Marina Mandarin Singapore. These gigantic structures transform the space around them, changing the massing of the area. Another influential architect working in this style was Paul Rudolph, who received the important and prestigious commission for the new Art and Architecture Building at Yale University, New Haven, Connecticut (1963).

A HUMAN SCALE?

In the United Kingdom, architects like Basil Spence created new landmarks in concrete, including large, public-sector housing blocks. These soon became associated with social problems, however, and came to seem too impersonal in scale.

FUTURISM/GOOGIE

One of the broad design trends in the second half of the twentieth century was Futurism, which was an attempt, through architecture, to imagine the future. Like many recent styles, it had its roots in earlier twentieth-century design.

STYLE FILE

Notable Features:
High-tech materials;
Mechanized environment
(e.g., the "drive-thru");
Bold shapes, especially
curvilinear forms;
Streamlined, smooth,
aerodynamic lines;
Starbursts and neon.

Major Influences:
Technological advances.

Where and When:
Western United States,
Florida; 1955 onward.

OPPOSITE: *The Transamerica Pyramid (top) and Space Needle.* BELOW: *The Oriental Pearl TV Tower (1995), a Futurist icon in fast-growing Shanghai, China.*

The Metropolis Meets Googie

The writings and drawings of Italian architect Antonio Sant'Elia before 1916, and the Turin Futurists of the early 1920s and '30s, envisioned an interconnected, mechanized modern metropolis. This thread, when married to the car culture and Space Age emerging in 1940s' America, sparked what was called "Googie" or "Populuxe" architecture, found mostly in southern California, which lasted well into the 1960s. As post-World War II America enthusiastically embraced the idea of a fabulous technological, futuristic new age, Googie architecture became the rage for popular design. Cars sported larger and more flamboyant fins, and the architecture of ubiquitous coffee shops, bowling alleys, and motels matched them with sweeping roofs, curvy geometric shapes, bold glass, steel features, and dazzling neon. The American obsession with space travel spurred this trend, which spread to places like Las Vegas and Miami, Florida. Upswept roofs and starbursts were essential to the style; perhaps the best-known example of the starburst is the

"Welcome to Fabulous Las Vegas" sign seen in so many movies. The Space Needle that was built for Seattle's World Fair in 1962 is probably the most readily recognized Googie-inspired architectural landmark.

Spaceships and Wings

One of the progenitors of the Futurist style was California's William L. Pereira, whose Encounter Restaurant (1997), in the Theme Building at the Los Angeles airport, is a structurally unique building resembling a space spider, complete with UFOs in the form of fantastically bright exterior lamps. The restaurant rests atop a 70-foot pillar nestled among the "spider legs." Another of his California landmarks is the Transamerica Pyramid in San Francisco (1969–72), then the tallest building west of the Mississippi River. Its spire is covered in aluminum panels, and the top of the pyramid supports "wings."

NEW IN FUTURISM

Current Futurism has been reinterpreted by a new generation of architects. Carlos A. Ott created a new home for the Opéra Bastille in Paris, commissioned to commemorate the 200th anniversary of the French Revolution instigated at the site. The Arthur Erickson practice designed a fantastic, twisted tower for Ritz-Carlton in Vancouver, Canada, set to open in 2009, but the project was canceled after Erickson's death.

EXPRESSIONISM

The Expressionist style was very similar to the Modernist and Brutalist styles and shares many of the same roots. All were concerned with pure, geometric forms, but where Modernists veered toward austerity in design, Expressionists tried to elicit an emotional response through sculptured forms.

ABOVE: *The Air Force Academy Chapel (1963), Colorado Springs, Colorado (Skidmore, Owings, and Merrill).*
BELOW: *Eero Saarinen's TWA Flight Center (1962, now T5) at John F. Kennedy International Airport, New York City.*

Freedom of Expression

Some of the twentieth century's most memorable buildings were designed by Expressionist architects—and they are so memorable precisely because they strike a resonant emotional chord. Provoking controversy, as well as emotion, was the Sydney Opera House, Sydney, Australia, whose design was awarded to Danish architect Jørn Utzon in 1957. During the sixteen years it took to complete the project, political intrigues and a firestorm of criticism from the hostile Australian press drove Utzon to resign: he never even saw his completed masterpiece. The building was finished by other designers under the supervision of Peter Hall. Since its opening in 1973, it has become the world's busiest performing-arts center—and a national emblem of Australia.

Father and Son

Eero Saarinen is another architect who infused his work with enormous emotion. In a 1947 competition that his father, Eliel, had also entered, Saarinen was awarded the design of the Jefferson National Expansion Memorial, St. Louis, Missouri (1966), commemorating the Louisiana Purchase and westward movement in the United States. With utter, symmetrical simplicity (the arch is 630 feet high and 630 feet wide at its base), the Gateway Arch solicits a resounding emotional response while simultaneously exhibiting the glories of technology. The graceful, tapered curve of stainless steel is the tallest memorial in the United States.

Another of Saarinen's brilliant emotional statements is the 1962 Trans World Airlines (TWA) terminal at John F. Kennedy Airport, New York City, whose free-flowing curves and cantilevered form suggest a bird in flight, as well as the excitement of travel in the Jet Age.

THE FIFTH FACADE

The most striking and transporting aspect of the Sydney Opera House is the "fifth facade" of the shimmering roof, whose shapes were inspired by palm leaves. Apparently poised to set sail, the billowing roofline strikes a dramatic counterpoint to the coat-hanger shape of nearby Sydney Harbor Bridge. Through an ingenious use of concrete platforms, the complex of theaters and halls is linked beneath the spherical roof, with its shells sheathed in glittering white ceramic tiles.

BELOW: *Arguably Australia's most famous landmark, the Sydney Opera House.*

STRUCTURAL EXPRESSIONISM

Also sometimes called High-tech Modernism, this movement visibly exposed structural elements, on both the exterior and the interior, to express the aesthetic qualities of the building. The detailing remained similar to that of the International style, but larger design elements dominated through feats of engineering.

STYLE FILE

Notable Features:
Metallic elements;
Detached frames;
Exposed trussworks;
Complex shapes
  requiring imaginative
  engineering.

Major Influences:
International style;
Modernism;
Expressionism.

Where and When:
Worldwide; 1975 to the
present day.

BELOW: *Facade, structural, and pipes detail of the colorful Centre Georges Pompidou, Paris.*

The Pompidou Breakthrough

The most popular building in this style is Paris's galvanizing Centre Georges Pompidou (1976), designed by Richard Rogers Partnership. The most daring and innovative feature of the building was the location of the essential services on the exterior. But this was not purely for visual effect: it allowed for uncluttered gallery spaces suffused with light within the museum. The architects reprised this technique for the Lloyds Building (London, 1986). Centre Georges Pompidou also represented a change in the urban planning of public spaces. An equal amount of space was given over to public areas of open-air theatres, cafés, and stores. To further accommodate the public and pedestrians and make this a popular destination, three of the surrounding streets were closed to automobile traffic.

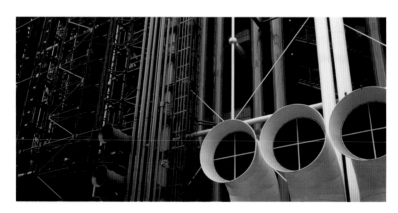

LEFT: *The HSBC headquarters building in Hong Kong's Statue Square. Designed by Norman Foster and completed in 1985, this structure echoes others in this style in having no central core; built with bridge engineering, its supporting structure (as well as all its services) is external, allowing for unobstructed internal floor space. Natural light provides most of its illumination, a trend that has become more popular in the subsequent decades.*

Outside the Box

While the Pompidou Center was one of the first Structural Expressionist buildings to have its vertical circulation pipes on the exterior, buildings are still being designed and constructed in this style, and with this feature. Foster and Partners, headed by Norman Foster, a world leader of the style, designed Deutsche Bank Place in Sydney, Australia, which was completed in 2005. Another practitioner of the style, although more naturalistic, is Santiago Calatrava, whose Turning Torso (2005), in Malmö, Sweden (*see* page 255), twists a full 90 degrees from bottom to top and is reminiscent of many forms occurring in nature—a twisting torso, or strand of DNA. This innovative building houses both office space and residential apartments and is constructed in nine "cubes" of five stories, with one story between each cube. It is also designed with the environment in mind: each apartment is equipped with a consumption monitor to control energy usage and costs.

COLOR CODES

What makes the Pompidou Center instantly recognizable is the use of bold primary colors for the external services, which correspond to industry-standard color codes. The electrical system is yellow, the water services are blue, the elevators and circulation systems are red, and the air conditioning is blue or white. Also mounted on the exterior are several escalators in tiered glass tubes, affording passengers stunning views of Paris, and providing visual movement for viewers of the building itself.

CONTEMPORARY MODERNISM

Modernism at its most elegant is exemplified in the work of one of the last century's most celebrated architects, I.M. (Ieoh Ming) Pei, in whose work can be seen the spare aesthetics of the Bauhaus (*see* pages 228–29) and Modernist (*see* pages 240–41) movements, but also culturally sensitive—even romantic—design.

STYLE FILE

Notable Features:
Abstract, geometric shapes;
References to historical precedents;
Complex or high-tech structural design;
Plain surfaces, especially of glass and other reflective materials;
Feature skylights.

Major Influences:
Bauhaus;
International Style;
Modernism.

Where and When:
Major cities worldwide; 1970s onward.

Icon of Abstraction

Born in China, Pei studied in the United States, for a time under Walter Gropius at Harvard. His buildings combine abstract shapes with simple, elegant finishes, creating monuments of huge cultural importance. The East Wing of the National Gallery of Art (1974–78), Washington, D.C., which houses the United States' modern and contemporary art collection, is noted for its exquisite siting and breathtakingly expansive interior spaces. Pei made beautiful accommodations for the building and its visitors: there are wide pedestrian walkways to manage the traffic patterns within the exhibition halls. In what has become his signature, there is an underground passageway with glazed, pyramidal skylights.

The Glass Ceiling

At the Louvre (*see* feature, left) Pei solved the problem of grafting a modern design onto an historic landmark with a glass pyramid, its proportions based on the ancient wonder at Giza. He surrounded this new main entrance (which is capable of admitting 15,000 people an hour) with three small pyramids and three reflecting pools, placing it in the center of the Napoleon Court, with the U-shaped Louvre around it. The main pyramid is a complex, interlinked steel structure sheathed in reflective glass; its genius is in the sheer simplicity of its form. The translucent pyramid is of its time, but refers to the ancient world; it defers to the larger presence of the surrounding building by literally reflecting it. It was what Pei claimed to be "a natural solution."

OPPOSITE: *Detail view of the Louvre Pyramid, Paris, France.*

RIGHT: *The 790-foot Hancock Tower, Boston (1972–76), was designed by I.M. Pei with his partner, Henry Cobb.*

POSTMODERNISM

While Postmodernism evolved from Modernism, it did so in opposition to that style, which was eventually seen as sterile, anonymous, too universal, and lacking meaning. Postmodernist buildings are designed to be unique and surprising, and are a blend of traditional, contemporary, and newly invented elements, often blending numerous styles in a single building.

STYLE FILE

Notable Features:
A blend of features from
  disparate styles;
Surprising contrasts, e.g.,
  of new and old styles;
Humor, wit, and whimsy.

Major Influences:
Modernism;
Historical styles,
  especially Classical;
Local design traditions.

Where and When:
Worldwide; 1960 onward.

"Less Is a Bore"

Architect Robert Venturi's famous criticism "Less is a bore" referred to the featureless monotony that he perceived in modern design. Architects like Michael Graves, Ricardo Bofill, and Aldo Rossi were concerned with context and tradition, but also with a winking whimsy and humor. They sought to combine new ideas with traditional forms. A perfect example of this blend is the AT&T Building (1978–84, now the Sony Building), by Modernist-turned-Postmodernist Philip Johnson. The sleek skyscraper is topped by an outrageous pink-granite neo-Georgian (Chippendale) pediment.

RIGHT: *Michael Graves's library (1982) at San Juan Capistrano, California, was based on the Spanish Mission architecture of the area, with cream-colored stucco surfaces and red roof tiles. The building is organized around a courtyard and has covered walkways and roofed outdoor reading areas.*

LEFT: *Graves's Humana Building (1985) in Louisville, Kentucky, stands between historic buildings and modern high-rises. Critics of Graves's work have sneered at his populist designs, which are scattered with Classical mementoes or witty allusions, as nothing more than vulgar kitsch, but this building style remains immensely popular.*

FUN AND GAMES

Michael Graves's fantastical Dolphin and Swan hotels at the Walt Disney resort in Florida (1989–90) are playful in the extreme. The Dolphin Hotel is a turquoise-and-coral pyramid. On top are two 56-foot dolphins; water cascades down the side into a giant clamshell. The Swan Hotel has a gently curving roofline topped by a pair of 47-foot swans. There are hand-painted murals on the exterior walls, and the two hotels are joined by a sheltered walkway over a lagoon. This is architecture as entertainment, with every intention of delighting the viewer.

Wit and Wisdom

The strict dogma of Modernism gave way to a more playful and ironic use of decoration and historical quotation. When asked to design a large extension to the Allen Art Museum at Oberlin College, Ohio (1973–76), a Tuscan Renaissance building by Cass Gilbert, Venturi made reference to the original building by using the same red sandstone and pink granite, but in a checkerboard pattern on the facade. As a counterpoint to the original pavilion's symmetry, the extension is asymmetrically joined. In a small, rear alcove is a massively exaggerated wooden column with a giant Ionic capital, a perfect example of Postmodernist wit. The work of Michael Graves epitomizes the Postmodern exuberance in design and the use of stylistic references. He borrows all manner of historical detailing for his designs, which are meant to be whimsical and entertaining (*see* feature).

DECONSTRUCTIVISM

Once it became more commercialized in the building boom of the 1980s, the novelty of Postmodernism wore off, and it seemed banal. The path was clear for Deconstructivism to emerge: controversial, different, a "new way of seeing."

STYLE FILE

Notable Features:
Nonlinear design process;
Asymmetric and non-geometric appearance;
Impressions of fragmentation;
Unpredictable appearances;
Complex engineering, using CAD software in design and building;
Montage technique;
Exposed structural elements.

Major Influences:
Modernism;
Constructivism.

Where and When:
Worldwide; 1980 onward.

Dissolving the Limits

This radical style explodes a building into a loose collection of related fragments, pulling apart the basic elements of built structures. Its architects challenge the fundamental precepts of building design and geometry. According to Deconstructivist architect Bernard Tschumi, it is "part of a research into the dissolving limits of architecture." As well as having roots in Modernism, the style refers to Constructivism (*see* pages 218–19), which turned away from the classic notion in architecture that balanced forms create a unified whole. Deconstructivists put pieces together in such nonstandard ways that they achieve wildly skewed compositions. The ordered and the rational—even the right angle—give way, so that the buildings may appear dismantled, fractured, fragmented, or unbalanced.

OPPOSITE, ABOVE: *British Iraqi Zaha Hadid's 2002 ski jump at Bergisel, Innsbruck, Austria, extends the topography of the slope into the sky.*
OPPOSITE, BELOW: *Santiago Calatrava's irregular pentagonal "Turning Torso" (see also page 249) in Malmö, Sweden.*
RIGHT: *China Central Television Headquarters, Beijing. Designed by Rem Koolhaas and Ole Scheeren, and completed in 2009, the building is an irregular loop of six sections.*

No Right Angles

Theorists like Rem Koolhaas and Peter Eisenman set out to change the way we look at, think about, and use space. Unlike the Modernists, they do not adhere to the ideal of a "pure" form; instead, they consider that impurity is inherent. With glass floors, erratic, zigzagging stairs, and shimmering translucent walls, Koolhaas seems to use technology to demonstrate new ways to live. For Eisenman, a

key element of good design is "the uncanny." He aims to create a sense of unease, as well as a sense of what is absent; he wants us to look not just at the surface, but at the "in between." A former student of Koolhaas who became a partner in his London-based firm, Zaha Hadid became in 2004 the first woman to win the Pritzker Architecture Prize. She is widely acclaimed for her designs, which incorporate strong, sweeping forms and streamlined geometric structures.

Feats of Engineering

As in many previous architectural movements, major advances in construction technology had to be made in order for some Deconstructivist buildings to be possible. The almost shocking simplicity of the asymmetrical Erasmus Bridge (Ben van Berkel, 1996) in Rotterdam, the Netherlands, would be impossible without state-of-the-art engineering. The sinuous arc is entirely suspended from a single, soaring pylon 450 feet high and becomes a new point of orientation in Rotterdam, joining the old part of the city to the new across the Maas River.

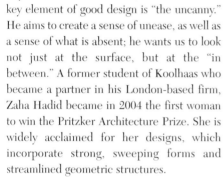

FRANK GEHRY

Sharing many of its defining characteristics, "starchitect" Frank Owen Gehry's work is often described as Deconstructivist. Despite having a signature look, however, Gehry has reinvented his work so often that it defies labeling.

STYLE FILE

Notable Features:
Inspired by fine art and organic forms;
Nonlinear modeling;
CATIA design process;
Impressions of fragmentation;
Chaotic appearances;
Montage technique;
Use of novel materials: titanium, corrugated aluminum, stainless steel, and chain link;
Imaginative use of internal space.

Major Influences:
Deconstructivism;
Contemporary artists and sculptors.

Where and When:
Worldwide; distinctive style from the 1980s.

Back to Nature

Frank Gehry (b. 1929) has a unique approach to architecture that owes more to contemporary art and to inspirations found in nature (most notably, fish shapes) than to the traditions of his profession. He strives to translate emotion into his structures, to evoke passions through them, and to bring them to life with reflected light dancing on undulating surfaces. Starting with conceptual sketches, he achieves his radical forms by modeling, initially with found objects and crumpled paper, working up successive models until the desired look is achieved. Finally, the working models are scanned using CATIA (3D software originally developed for military uses). The computer simulation is used not only at the design stage, but in the cutting of materials and at all stages of construction.

RIGHT: *Surface details of the Frederick R. Weisman Museum of Art (1991), at the University of Minneapolis, Minnesota (near right); and the "Ginger and Fred" building, Prague, Czech Republic (far right, see feature).*
OPPOSITE, LEFT: *Interior view of the renovations to the Art Gallery of Ontario in Toronto, Canada, Gehry's city of origin.*
OPPOSITE, RIGHT: *Gehry's best known work, the Guggenheim Museum Bilbao, Spain.*

Pop Goes the Past

First coming to the attention of critics through the extraordinary 1977 chain-link, corrugated-metal addition for his own California home, Gehry became an overnight celebrity with the opening of his Guggenheim Museum Bilbao, Spain (1991–97). Its abstract, sculptural form boasts not a single flat surface; its steel frame is largely covered in paper-thin, highly reflective titanium sheathing, which ripples in the wind. Critics quickly declared it a masterpiece.

Appearances Deceive

Gehry's work has always drawn detractors, who claim that it is architecture designed to shock, but ignores functional needs and aesthetics. Nevertheless, his projects are much more practical than they might at first appear. Unlike many landmarks, they have almost always been delivered within budget and on schedule. Perhaps even more importantly, end-users consistently enthuse about the experience of inhabiting Gehry's imaginative spaces. No architect has achieved such universal acclaim since Frank Lloyd Wright.

GINGER AND FRED: SHALL WE DANCE?

Officially known as the Nationale-Nederlanden building, this 1997 anthropomorphic Prague landmark was the result of a collaboration between Gehry and Vlado Milunic. "Fred" is animated by a wavy, bas-relief pattern on curving wall planes and appears gracefully poised in embrace with his flaring, glazed partner.

BLOBITECTURE

Architecture has always evolved to take advantage of new technologies. In recent decades, extensive use of computer modeling has created several new architectural phenomena, among them being the "blob." While a blob may be imagined as relatively low-tech, creating one is an extremely challenging task.

STYLE FILE

Notable Features:
Amorphous or globular, rounded shapes;
Usually made of glass, stainless steel, and synthetic building materials.

Major Influences:
Organic architecture;
Deconstructivism

Where and When:
Worldwide; mid-1990s to the present day.

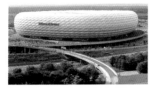

ABOVE: *The Allianz Arena in Munich, Germany, designed by the firm Herzog & de Meuron. It opened in 2005 and was used as a venue in the 2006 soccer World Cup.*
RIGHT: *The Sage Gateshead, designed by Foster and Partners, opened in 2004.*
OPPOSITE: *Detail of Selfridges (opened 2003) in Birmingham, England, designed by the Future Systems practice.*

How to Build a Blob

The simple name is deceptive: designing and building a blob requires extensive computer modeling and innovative construction techniques. Blobs are designed using sophisticated computer-aided design (CAD) programs. Architects manipulate the algorithms of the modeling program to create new, fluid forms. Translating these amorphous designs into physical reality presents further challenges, as steel, glass, and synthetic polymers are molded into unfamiliar shapes. Blobitecture is so far confined to the urban, public sphere, partly because the building materials commonly used do not afford much privacy. The first completely computer-designed blob was the Water Pavilion in the Netherlands; another "blobby" feature pioneered in this work is the interactive interior, which responds with light and sound to the visitors inside.

Above: *London's bulbous City Hall, designed by Norman Foster, was opened in 2002. Like Frank Lloyd Wright's Guggenheim Museum, New York (see page 238), it has an internal helical walkway.*

THE BRAIN BLOB

The Philological Library at the Free University of Berlin is a wonderful example of Blobitecture. Designed by Norman Foster and completed in 2005, the library bears a resemblance to the human brain, with the rounded shape and grayish color. The form pays homage to the intellectually challenging design process, as well as the function of the building.

Best of Blobs

The twenty-first century has seen some outstanding examples of the Blobitecture style, including London's City Hall and the Sage Gateshead musical center in northeast England. Despite considerable variation in form, many blob buildings share a preference for curving, fluid lines and light-filled, interactive interiors. The rounded, flowing silhouettes offer a sharp contrast to the strict geometry and straight lines that had defined architecture for centuries. Such shapes are made possible by the CAD programs, which automatically calculate the equations for structural soundness.

ORGANIC

Organic architecture aims to integrate space into a unified whole. This includes the setting: a building should "grow" naturally from its environment, using local materials and reflecting its cultural as well as natural situation.

Wright's Disciples

Australian architects in the 1950s and '60s were inspired to translate Wright's vision of organic architecture (*see* pages 232–33) to the Bush. They created homes from natural materials that not only take advantage of the terrain, but enhance it. Demonstrating that the building should be part of the site, not just placed on it, these homes exhibit free massing, exposed timber structure, and textured brickwork with a horizontal emphasis that mirrors the horizontal emphasis of the roof planes. They employed shapes that either complement the site or can be found in the building's natural surroundings. Since the 1970s these architects have developed their ideas further to address energy efficiency and sustainability. Organic architect Anton Alberts, known for his ING Building (1982), Amsterdam, the Netherlands, was also influenced by the anthroposophic architecture of Rudolf Steiner, which had a more spiritual than environmental inspiration.

OPPOSITE, TOP: *The Scottish Parliament building, Edinburgh, entrance and facade details, with oak, stone, and concrete. Several connected, low-lying buildings incorporate a variety of Scottish motifs, from leaves and boats to figures drawn from art.*
RIGHT: *"Te Papa": the National Museum of New Zealand, in Wellington, makes extensive use of local motifs and materials.*

"Surging out of the Rock"

Completed in 2004, the Scottish Parliament Building in Edinburgh was designed by Catalan architect Enric Miralles (1955–2000) to house the newly independent Scottish government. Miralles wanted the building to "reflect the land it represents" and to "surge out of the rock" (the nearby peak of Arthur's Seat) as well as to reference Scottish culture.

Similarly, the Hungarian architect Imre Makovecz, a current champion of organic architecture, designs buildings to work with the natural surroundings rather than triumph over them and to refer to Hungarian art and the architectural history of his sites. The Stephaneum at the Pázmány Péter Catholic University, Piliscaba (1995), is a sculptural montage of joined, almost collapsed-looking, buildings with different architectural styles and representations of different myths. There is an enchanting colonnade of molded plaster in the form and colors of the forest; man-sized capitals flank the entrance to the auditorium. His theater in Mako, Hungary (1996), sometimes called the "Onion Building," recreates the local medieval townscape.

METABOLIST BUILDINGS

A group of Japanese designers came together in the 1950s to form the Metabolist movement. They championed the use of prefabricated units that could be arranged flexibly, promoting the organic growth of urban buildings. Kisho Kurokawa's Nakagin Capsule Tower (1972, pictured below), comprised 140 units of living and office space. Its popularity was limited, however.

CONTEMPORARY TRENDS

Contemporary architecture continues to push the boundaries of materials and technology in the quest for creative expression and for solutions to tomorrow's problems. Demographics, climate change, emerging economies, and scarcity of resources have combined to place sustainability firmly at the center of the design agenda.

MEGACITIES

Defined as a metropolis with a population exceeding 10 million, the megacity is a 21st-century phenomenon. Asia already has fourteen (pictured below: Mumbai, India), the largest of which being Tokyo, Japan (the world's largest at approximately 34 million inhabitants). Mexico City is the biggest city in the Americas (third-largest in the world), while Moscow, Russia, is Europe's most populous city. In 1800, just 3 percent of the world's population were city dwellers; in 2008 the United Nations estimated that more than half of all people lived in cities.

The Need for Solutions

The world's population is growing at an escalating rate and becoming increasingly urbanized (*see* feature, left). Concern about exhausting the planet's natural and mineral resources and the impact of climate change on drought and flooding puts pressure on planners and architects to find new ways of building for this ever-increasing population.

The search for inexpensive, quickly built houses as the population grows has led to many innovations in construction engineering. The Quonset Hut, created in response to military needs during World War II, with its floor and continuous half-cylinder walls of corrugated metal, had a powerful impact on domestic architecture after the war. Prefabrication was a solution for its time, but by now it is evident that far more radical thinking is necessary. But should we build higher, to relieve land density? Or smaller, so that people consume less space and fewer resources? Or are different materials required, or should we be more radical still in our approach?

Top: *The Tumbleweed Tiny House Company, California, specializes in compact, energy-efficient living spaces.*

Domes, Modules, and More

Richard Buckminster Fuller, motivated by a desire to benefit humankind, set about experimenting with ways of "doing more with less." Most famously, this took the form of the geodesic dome, the centerpiece of the American Pavilion at Expo '67, the world's fair held in Montreal, Canada. Fuller based his dome on his theories of "energetic-synergetic geometry," and it was seen as another possible solution to the postwar world housing shortage. But it was unsuitable for domestic use: it provides little usable living space and no obvious place for utilities. The dome was popular in commercial applications, however, including the Epcot Center in Orlando, Florida, and the Eden Project, Cornwall, England, which consists of several enclosed biospheres.

Some have seen the idea of building self-contained, isolated "biomes" in inhospitable terrain—hostile climates, or even in space—as a potential avenue for future development. Others, like innovator Rachel Armstrong, have looked to nature rather than technology. Armstrong proposes that "inert, Victorian technologies" give way to the use of biological matter as building materials, so that structures could, hypothetically, repair themselves, as well as being inherently sustainable.

SMALL IS BEAUTIFUL, MODULAR IS MODEST

Modular housing and prefabrication have been around in the United States since the 1890s, when houses were sold out of mail-order catalogs as soon as the cross-country railroad was completed. Prefabrication and modular building picked up after World War II and helped reduce some of the ensuing housing shortage.

Trailer parks and mobile homes may come to mind when we think of prefabricated homes, but this industry has changed dramatically, and prefabricated homes are offered in every size and style.

In Japan, as we have seen (page 261), the Metabolists tried to popularize pod- or cell-based design, and although they achieved only limited success, new versions of this idea are under development today.

Another trend that stems from sustainable architecture is that of building small. Bucking the "bigger is better" trend and rejecting the "McMansions" of the 1980s and '90s, tiny homes are now in vogue, some of them hand-crafted and carbon neutral.

LEFT: *Conoidal dome detail at the Mitchell Park Horticultural Center, Milwaukee, Wisconsin.*

Higher and Higher

Ever since the first skyscrapers were conceived and built, we have had an architectural love affair with height. Engineering and technological advances mean that we can climb higher and higher into the sky. The nonprofit Council on Tall Buildings and Urban Habitat, arbiter of the world's tallest buildings, measures a building from the sidewalk level of the main entrance to the structural top. This does not include antennas or flagpoles, but "structural" does not have to mean "functional," which is why the Petronas Towers complex, Kuala Lumpur, Malaysia (1996), at 88 stories is considered taller than the Sears Tower, Chicago, Illinois (1974-76), with its 110 stories.

The Twin Towers at the World Trade Center (1973), New York City, by Minoru Yamasaki, were meant to symbolize both the global economy centered on New York's financial district and—perhaps less well-known at the time—world peace. At 1,353 feet, they were the tallest towers in the world upon completion, but were soon stripped of that title by Chicago's Sears Tower. Terrorist targets because they were such potent and totemic symbols, they were brought down in the attacks of September 11, 2001.

The height race used to be concentrated on New York and Chicago: Frank Lloyd Wright even drew up plans for a mile-high building for Chicago. But more recently, towers and skyscrapers in Asia and the Middle East have been claiming the limelight. Skyscrapers are seen as prestigious proof of economic might. The prosperity and ambition of a city or nation are imposed on these monumental landmarks, symbols of national pride and development. As developing nations come to the economic fore in the global market, their skylines are growing to match.

THE TWIN TOWERS

"The World Trade Center should, because of its importance, become a living representation of man's belief in humanity, his need for individual dignity, his belief in the cooperation of men, and through this cooperation his ability to find greatness."
—Minoru Yamasaki

BELOW: *The Sears tower, Chicago, long-time record holder and the first skyscraper of bundled-tube design (highly effective in withstanding wind).*

LEFT: *The Burj Khalifa, Dubai, United Arab Emirates. Dubai became known for architectural risk-taking and innovation during the first decade of the twenty-first century, when it experienced an extraordinary construction boom.*

RECORD BREAKERS

The tallest freestanding structure in the world is the Burj Khalifa (formerly known as the Burj Dubai), in the United Arab Emirates. Far surpassing the height of its nearest competitors, it reaches a soaring 2,684 feet, or 2,717 feet (828m) including its spire. Reputed to have cost around US$1.5 bn to construct, it was opened to great fanfare at the start of 2010 — unfortunately during the deepest world recession since the 1930s.

The next-tallest free-standing structure is the CN Tower, by John Andrews, located in Toronto, Canada. Completed in 1976, the tower is 1,815 feet, with its Space Deck observation platform at a dizzying 1,465 feet.

Runner-up to the Burj Khalifa as the next-tallest permanently occupied structure in the world is the Shanghai World Financial Center, which reaches a height of 1,614 feet and has an observation deck at 1,555 feet. It opened in 2008.

A Mile High: Nightmare or Dream?

In the fearful aftermath of September 11, structural engineers scrambled to strengthen existing buildings, and there was a hiatus in tall building. That hiatus is now over. Fantastically tall buildings require extremely sturdy materials and deep, fortified bases; elaborate cranes and pumping systems are needed to get materials and concrete up to the top levels, and the prevailing wisdom indicates that buildings net an economic loss above fifty stories due to the space needed for elevator shafts and steel reinforcements cutting down on rentable square footage. Some engineering experts feel that the current technology could support mile-high buildings (5,280 feet), but that the real limitation is money. Others are of the opinion that engineering developments in lighter, stronger materials, faster elevators, and advanced sway dampers are needed before we build higher, but that mile-high cities will be possible, housing millions or more. As always with skyscrapers, it is a case of "watch this space."

Above: *The Jin Mao Tower in Shanghai, China, was designed by the Chicago office of Skidmore, Owings, and Merrill, and construction was completed in 1998. Like the Petronas Towers in Malaysia, the building's proportions are designed around the number eight, which is associated with prosperity.*

Right: *Central Plaza, Hong Kong, was the tallest building in Asia from 1992 to 1996.*

LEFT: *Daniel Libeskind's Imperial War Museum North in Manchester, England, consists of three shards representing earth, air, and water. Symbolizing conflict, the building (2000–2) was intended to resonate emotionally with visitors. (Many members of Libeskind's family lost their lives in the Holocaust.)*

Going Greener

Sustainable architecture attempts to balance the needs of present and future societies to maintain acceptable standards of living with the capacity of the environment to fulfill those needs. Green designers share some principles with the organic architects, but take the idea farther beyond the aesthetics. In practical terms, the architect makes an effort to lessen a building's impact on the environment through energy and resource efficiency, which includes trying to eliminate or minimize the use of toxins and to reduce energy consumption during preparation and building.

Before opting for new construction, architects will first try to reuse, adapt, or extend existing structures or else reuse materials for new works, and when they do build, they seek to create environmentally friendly, energy-efficient structures by effectively managing natural resources. This includes incorporating solar or ground energy and materials that in their manufacture, application, and disposal do the least possible harm to the air, water, and site, and considering carbon capture. There is also an effort to create buildings that are conducive to the health and well-being of their occupants, and a drive to support pedestrians, cyclists, and the use of mass transit in urban-planning designs.

WHY SUSTAINABLE?

A number of factors have contributed to the movement promoting an environmentally friendly, socially responsible ethos for architecture. These include:

Fears that the planet is almost catastrophically overpopulated;

Dwindling supplies of basic construction and utility materials;

Overexploitation of natural resources and our proximity to Peak Oil, making new approaches essential;

Climate change;

The hole in the ozone layer created by our use of harmful chemicals;

Extinct or endangered species and shrinking biodiversity;

The scarcity and poor quality of water in some regions, coupled with devastating, repeated flooding in others.

THE GREEN ROOF: A GROWING TREND

THE GREEN ROOF: A GROWING TREND

A recent trend in sustainable design, based on ancient indigenous precedents, is the "green roof." In order to reduce energy consumption through heat loss, decrease storm-water runoff, and preserve the life of roofing materials, drought-resistant plants are incorporated into covers that are placed over an existing roof. An additional advantage of this socially responsible solution is that these roofs can also replace some of the green spaces that are sacrificed in the building process, especially in urban areas.

Learning From the Past

Another sustainable strategy is to revive traditional methods of building, usually employing renewable materials. Adapted from ancient precedents, stabilized rammed earth is a wall material that can be finished to look like stone, matching the strength of concrete and the weather-resistance of brick. Bamboo is fast-growing and strong, while coconut, sisal, grass, and straw bales are all feasible wall or roofing materials, and green roofs have further benefits (*see* feature). Gabions—cages or boxes filled with sand, rubble, or similar, normally seen in military applications—have been used in several large projects.

The growing popularity of sustainable architecture is due in part to the fact that these structures tend to last longer and cost less to operate and maintain. Even if commercial building has been slower to embrace sustainable principles, there is every effort in new construction, sometimes mandated by law or encouraged through local taxation policy, to accommodate and promote greater energy efficiency. But the rising cost of energy has perhaps been the decisive factor in encouraging energy-saving innovations like passive solar design (also known as Passiv Haus), biomass, and ground-energy capture.

RIGHT: *Grass-roofed houses at a folk museum, Iceland. The Nordic countries, Greenland, and the Faroe Islands all have plenty of traditional examples of this practice. Inset above, detail of the green roof at City Hall in Chicago, Illinois.*

BUILDING ON CHALLENGING SITES

Problems with urban overcrowding and soaring land costs demand increasingly creative solutions. Designed by multiaward-winning Japanese architect Shuhei Endo, this 690-square-foot residence in Kobe, named "Rooftecture S," is sited on a once-forgotten embankment lot, clinging to the side of a coastal road. "Rooftecture" is described by Endo as a method by which architectural space is created from a continuous band. Here, the upper surface of corrugated steel folds over to form the building's seafront facade. This 66-foot-long site tapers in width from 13 feet to a blunt 5-foot point. Although strikingly contemporary, the residence contains a *doma*, or *toriniwa*: a traditional Japanese work space that at one time would have contained the kitchen and also served as a passageway to the rear of the building.

Greek-American MIT scientist Nicholas Negroponte coined the term "responsive architecture" in the 1960s. It was more or less synonymous with "smart" architecture, in which lighting and other functions were fully automated, controlled by computers—as seen in museums that house light-sensitive exhibits, for example. But more recently, "kinetic," or "dynamic," architecture has emerged. More than just having robotic services, parts of a building (such as individual stories) may move independently of one another, following, for example, the movement of the sun. The building thus constantly changes shape. Jose Leonidas Mejia and David Fisher are among the innovators in this field, David Fisher having masterminded the self-powered Da Vinci Tower whose plans were unveiled in 2008 for construction in Dubai.

OPPOSITE, TOP: *The Tate Modern, London.*

OPPOSITE, BELOW: *The Egg, or the National Center for Performing Arts (2001–7), Beijing, China, designed by French architect Paul Andreu.*

New Uses for Old Buildings

The staggering cost of new construction, especially in congested urban areas, frequently leads to the conversion of old buildings into new public attractions, particularly when landmark buildings are protected from demolition. Many handsome nineteenth-century banks have been converted into eateries, clubs, and other businesses.

The low availability of housing stock in high-density, inner-city areas has prompted conversion of former industrial and commercial areas for residential use. Starting in the 1980s the former factories and warehouses of the SoHo and TriBeCa areas of New York City were transformed into lofts, and an entire style of fashionable domestic architecture was born. A parallel movement began in rural areas, where barns were converted into loftlike living spaces.

Some buildings are beloved cultural treasures, and adaptive reuse is a solution when the original use becomes outdated. In 1898, Victor Laloux, the Beaux Arts architect, won the competition for the Gare d'Orsay station and hotel in Paris. It opened to great fanfare in time for the 1900 World's Fair and was a masterpiece of modernity and industry. Obsolete by 1939, it only served the suburbs because modern trains were too long for the platforms. By 1975 it was slated for demolition, but was saved to make a new home for French Impressionist and Post-Impressionist painting. The enormous barrel vault of iron and glass and glass awning were made the main features of the new Musée d'Orsay, which opened in 1986.

Another creative adaptive reuse was the transformation of the disused Bankside Power Station, London, England, originally designed by Sir Giles Gilbert Scott (who also designed the red British telephone box) into the Tate

Modern in 2000. The conversion was designed by Swiss architects Herzog & de Meuron. The exterior remained the same, with the exception of a two-story glass structure on top spanning the length of the building. Inside, the massive Turbine Hall was maintained to display enormous exhibits. The original design kept the chimney height below that of St. Paul's Cathedral, on the opposite bank of the River Thames, and the two buildings are now linked by the Millennium Bridge, making this a popular destination for residents and tourists alike.

What Next?

So what does the future hold? Biological building blocks? Shape-shifting structures that are dynamic rather than static? Superscrapers or tiny houses? All of the above? Only time will tell.

BRIDGING MILLENNIA

The Millennium Bridge opened on June 10, 2000, as London's first new Thames crossing in more than a century. The 1,050-foot-long structure was designed by Norman Foster. It has "lateral suspension," an innovation that allows bridges to be suspended without tall supporting columns.

GLOSSARY

abacus A slab on the top of the capital of a column.

acanthus leaf A stylized Mediterranean leaf form decoration, especially for Corinthian capitals.

acroterion A pedestal for a sculpture or ornament at the base or apex of a pediment.

adobe Sun-dried clay bricks or plaster used for building in warm, dry climates.

aisle The part of a church divided laterally from the nave by a row of pillars or columns.

amphitheater An oval or circular building with rising tiers of seats around an open space.

apex The point of culmination; the highest point.

apical Constituting an apex.

appliqué An ornament fastened to the surface or interior of a building.

apse A semicircular or vaulted projection from a church building, usually containing the sanctuary, or chancel, where the altar is located.

aqueduct A water-carrying bridge constructed almost entirely of a series of arches, often stacked in tiers.

arabesque A style of decoration involving complex patterns of stylized vegetal forms.

arcade A passageway with a roof supported by arched columns.

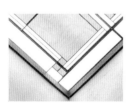

architrave The lower-most part of an entablature, resting directly atop a column in Classical architecture.

art glass A type of colored glass characterized by combinations of hues and special effects in transparency and opaqueness.

ashlar Square-cut stone laid in horizontal courses with vertical joints. Used as an alternative to brick. Generally the external face is smooth or polished, occasionally it is decorated by small grooves.

balloon framing A type of timber framing introduced in the mid-nineteenth century, in which the studs are continuous from sill to plate.

From top: An adobe wall; aisles divided from a central nave; an amphitheater; art glass; and a balustrade.

baluster A miniature column.

balustrade A row of balusters supporting a handrail, often used decoratively to frame or crown porches.

bargeboard Projecting boards, usually decorated, placed on the gable ends of a house.

barrack A building used to house military personnel.

barrel vault The most basic form of vault; essentially, an extended series of arches forming long, curved ceilings, semicircular in cross section.

basilica A rectangular building designed along a longitudinal axis, leading from a narthex through a central nave to an apse containing the sanctuary.

basilican plan Having a central nave flanked by aisles, as in a church.

batten A narrow strip of wood.

batter(ed) The upwardly receding slope of a wall or column.

bay The vertical sections projecting from a facade, usually featuring three or more windows.

belfry The part of a tower or steeple in which bells are hung.

bellcast roof A roof that flares out at the eaves.

belt course *See* string course.

belvedere A roofed structure, especially a small pavilion or tower on top of a building, situated so as to command a wide view.

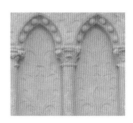

bent Preassembled sections of timber framing.

beveled Slanted.

blind arch An arch set against a wall, for decoration.

board-and-batten siding Alternating boards and thin strips of wood used to cover a building.

bow-truss roof Semicircular wooden roof.

brace A diagonal timber, straight or curved, that is mortised into two timbers set at right angles to each other to provide strength and rigidity.

bracket A small, projecting piece of stone or wood that supports a horizontal member.

broken pediment A pediment in which one or both cornices are not continuous.

buttress A masonry pier used for reinforcement of structural walls.

cable stays Heavy cables used to brace or support.

caming Metal framework for an art-glass window or panel, usually made of lead; also called "leading."

FROM TOP: A bargeboard; a belfry; blind arches; timber braces; and a cable-stay bridge.

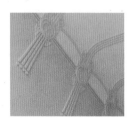

campanile A bell tower, especially one near, but not attached to, a church or other public building.

canales Water spouts.

candle snuffer A concave roof topping a rounded corner tower.

cantilever A projecting beam that is supported at only one end to form, e.g., a balcony.

capital The top part of a column, usually decorated, and larger than the column shaft.

cartouche A structure or figure, often in the shape of an oval shield or oblong scroll, used as an ornament or to bear a design or inscription.

caryatid An alternative to a column: a large female figure standing on a base, bearing the entablature on her head, and adorned with a capital.

casement window A narrow window with sashes that open outward on hinges.

castellated Having notched rooflines, or crenelations.

chink Any material used to fill narrow openings.

cladding A finishing material, like boards, shingles, or metal, overlaid on an unfinished wall or roof as weatherproofing.

clapboard A thin board laid horizontally and overlapped with others to form a weathertight surface on a wooden building.

clerestory A series of windows high in a wall.

closed-string stairway One in which the balusters do not rest on treads, but on a slanting footrail.

coffer A decorative, sunken panel, as in a ceiling, vault, or dome.

colonnade A row of columns with horizontal entablatures, such as friezes or sculptures.

column A supporting pillar consisting of a base, a cylindrical shaft, and a capital.

console An ornamental bracket.

coping The top layer of a masonry wall.

corbel A masonry block projecting from a wall to support a horizontal feature.

cornice A projecting feature, usually decorative, at the top of walls, arches, and eaves.

crenelation Notched rooflines of medieval origin, also called "battlements" for their original defensive function.

crepidoma The base on which a Classical temple sits.

cresting An ornamental ridge atop a wall or roof.

crocket A decorative roof ornament, usually leaf-shaped, common in Gothic Revival architecture.

cross vault *See* groin vault.

cruck framing A type of framing in which pairs of large, curved timbers, or crucks, rise from ground to rooftop, serving as both posts and main rafters.

cupola A small dome or other structure on a roof, commonly a belfry or for ventilation.

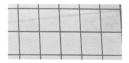

curtain wall A nonload-bearing, enclosing wall.

curvilinear Formed, bounded, or characterized by curved lines.

dendriform Resembling a tree in form and branching structure.

dentil One of a series of small, rectangular blocks forming a molding, or projecting beneath a cornice.

dogtrot A covered passageway between two parts of a building.

donjon A castle's tower, or keep.

dormer An upright window that projects from a sloping roof.

double-hung windows Having both sashes hung with weights and cords.

Dutch door Two-part door that allows for opening the upper and lower halves separately.

eaves The lower edge of a roof that projects beyond the wall below.

echinus An inverted, bell-shaped capital.

elbow A projection at the corner of an architrave; also, any small, projecting member or part of a piece or structure, either decorative or structural.

enclave A distinctly bounded area enclosed within a larger unit.

entablature The horizontal upper section of a Classical order, resting on the capital and including the architrave, frieze, and cornice.

FROM TOP: *Crenelation; a cupola; a skyscraper's glass curtain wall; dendriform columns; a dogtrot; and a Dutch door.*

FROM TOP: *A false front; a fanlight; a finial; flagstones; a gambrel roof; gingerbread decoration; and groin vaults.*

facade The face of a building, especially the principal face.

Fachwerk A German method of timber construction.

false front A rectangular, wooden facade that rises above the gable to mimic the flat-roofed appearance of Italianate-style structures.

fanlight A fan-shaped window or transom over a door.

fan vault A vault in which curving ribs radiate upward like a fan to form concave half-cones that meet, or nearly meet, at the apex.

fenestration The arrangement of the windows and/or doors of a house.

feng shui Ancient Chinese art of placement based on a philosophy of the movement of *chi*, or natural energy, through our environments.

finial A vertical ornament fixed to the peak of an arch or rooftop.

flagstone A flat slab of stone used as a paving material.

frame A building's supporting structure, or skeleton.

fretwork An ornamental feature consisting of three-dimensional, geometric designs or other symmetrical figures (frets) enclosed in a band or border.

frieze A decorative band around a wall, usually carved in relief.

gable The triangular area enclosed by the edges of a sloping roof. The gable ends are the walls under the gables (usually at the sides).

gambrel roof A ridged roof with two slopes on each side, the lower slope having the steeper pitch. Often seen on barns and neo-Dutch Colonial buildings.

geodesic dome A domed or vaulted structure of lightweight, straight, interlocking elements that form polygons.

gingerbread Informal name for ornate wooden decoration used on Victorian-style buildings.

Greek cross A popular, cruciform ground plan in which each arm is equal.

groin vault A vault formed by the intersection of two or more barrel vaults.

gypsum plaster Incorporates a type of chalk (gypsum) found in sedimentary rocks; also called plaster of Paris.

half-timbering A type of construction in which spaces formed by a timber frame are infilled with stone, brick, stucco, or wattle and daub, leaving part of the frame exposed.

hammerbeam roof A roof supported by short, horizontal and vertical beams, arranged like steps, bracing one another.

hardwood Description applied to woods from deciduous, broad-leafed trees.

helmet dome A small, steep-sided dome.

herringbone A pattern consisting of rows of short, slanted parallel lines, with the direction of the slant alternating row by row.

hex signs Ornamental, circular paintings with geometric or natural motifs on southeastern Pennsylvania barns built by Germans.

hip The angle formed by the meeting of two adjacent sloping sides of a roof.

hipped roof One on which the external angle is formed by the meeting of two adjacent sloping sides.

hood-molding An ornamental surround framing the upper part of a window.

horseshoe arch A round arch that widens before rounding off.

iconostasis A partition or screen separating the sanctuary from the main part of an Eastern Orthodox church, hung with icons, or sacred images.

inglenook A recessed area containing a fireplace with built-in seating on either side.

inlaid Decorated with veneers of fine materials set into the surface.

jetty An upper-story projection over the lower-story facade often seen in medieval-style buildings.

joists The parallel beams that support a floor or ceiling.

keep The stronghold of a castle.

keystone The central stone at the apex of an arch or vault.

FROM TOP: *Half-timbering; herringbone-laid bricks; hex signs; an iconostasis; and a jetty.*

lancet A narrow, pointed Gothic window.

leading *See* caming.

lean-to A structure with a single-pitched roof that is attached to the side of a building as a wing or an extension.

lintel The horizontal beam spanning the top of a door or window opening.

load-bearing Capable of carrying a load in addition to its own weight.

lobe A rounded projection that is part of a larger structure.

loggia A gallery or arcade open to the air on one or both sides.

loophole A vertical slot in a stone wall that provides air and light.

loshoes (long house) A connected building housing people in one section and livestock in the other.

lunette A semicircular window.

machicolation Projecting parapet with holes underneath.

mansard roof One having a double slope on all four sides, the lower slope being steeper than the upper, as seen in buildings of the French Empire style (named for the 17th-century French architect François Mansart).

massing The principal part of a structure.

mausoleum Large burial chamber, usually above ground.

medallion An oval or circular design used as decoration.

metope Any of the spaces between two triglyphs on a Doric frieze.

minaret A tall, slender tower attached to a mosque, having one or more projecting balconies.

mitered-glass windows Corner windows without supports or divisions.

moat A deep, water-filled trench.

modillion Plain, rectangular supports below a cornice line, indicating an extension of rafters through the wall.

FROM TOP: *Lancets; A lean-to; a loggia; a mansard roof; minarets; and a moat.*

mortise A notch cut into a piece of wood to receive a projecting part (tenon) shaped to fit.

mosaic A picture or decorative design made by setting small, colored pieces, as of stone or tile, into a surface.

mullion A slender, vertical bar between the panes of a window.

narthex The porch or entrance hall preceding the main hall in a place of worship.

nave The open, central space in a place of worship, often flanked by aisles and/or galleries.

niche An indented enclosure.

nogging Any material, including stone, brick, or wattle and daub, used to fill spaces between studs.

oculus (window) A circular window in the upper story or the dome of a building.

ogee arch An arch of two curves meeting at a point, as in Eastern architecture; also, a double curve with the shape of an elongated S.

onion dome A bulbous dome with a tapering tip.

order Columns or pilasters in various Greco-Roman styles, including Doric, Ionic, and Corinthian.

oriel window An upper-story bay window supported by a corbel or bracket.

padstone A large stone that supports a sill plate and rests immediately below a post to bear the building's weight.

pagoda Typically an east Asian, multistoried memorial structure or place of worhip.

palisade A protective wall of logs, sharp at one end.

parapet A low wall or railing along the edge of a roof or balcony.

parquet floor A floor covering of hardwood blocks laid in geometric patterns.

patio An outdoor space for dining or recreation that adjoins a residence and is often paved; also, a roofless inner courtyard, typically found in Spanish and Spanish-style dwellings.

pavilion On a facade, a prominent portion usually central or terminal, identified by projection, height, and special roof forms.

FROM TOP: *A mortise and tenon joint; an ogee arch; an onion dome; an oriel window; and a pagoda.*

From top: *A pendentive; a pilaster; a pinnacle; a porch; and a porte cochere.*

pear dome *See* onion dome.

pedestal urn A wide, shallow urn on a footed base, often used as a planter.

pediment A low, triangular element, framed by horizontal, sloping cornices, originating in Greek architecture and widely used as a design feature in Classical buildings, e.g., over doorways and windows.

pendant A gable ornament suspended from the roof peak, often flanked by bargeboards.

pendentives The triangular sections of vaulting between the rim of a dome and each adjacent pair of the arches that support it.

pentroof, pentice A small, single-sloped roof over a window, door, or other opening.

perforated Pierced.

pier A supporting post, usually square, shorter and thicker than a column.

pilaster A shallow, columnlike feature attached to a wall and often used to frame doorways and fireplaces.

pinnacle An ornament, originally forming the cap or crown of a buttress or small turret.

plate A horizontal timber connecting the tops of the outside posts of several bents and supporting the bases of the rafters.

Plexiglas A light, transparent, weather-resistant thermoplastic.

plinth *See* stylobate.

podium A low wall serving as a foundation. Also a wall circling the arena of an ancient amphitheater.

polychrome Made or decorated in many or various colors.

porch A covered platform, usually having a separate roof, at an entrance to a building.

portal A doorway, entrance, or gate, especially one that is large and imposing.

porte cochere A roof projecting over a driveway at the entrance to a building.

portico A covered porch or walkway supported by columns.

post-and-beam construction A basic building method that uses posts and beams to support a structure, with no load-bearing walls.

post-and-girt construction Timber-framing joined by hand-hewn notches.

post-and-lintel construction A system in which two upright members, the posts, hold up a third member, the lintel, laid horizontally across their top surfaces.

prefabricated Manufactured in advance, especially in standard sections that can be easily shipped and assembled.

pueblo A village, sometimes a simple, large, multi-family dwelling with stepped or terraced levels.

pulpit A raised platform.

quatrefoil An ornament composed of four clover-like lobes radiating from a common center and offset by triangular cusps between each lobe.

quoin A rectangle of stone, wood, or brick used in vertical series to decorate building corners and facade openings.

rectilinear Moving in, consisting of, bounded by, or characterized by a straight line or lines.

rib vault An arched area with slender supports; usually Romanesque and Gothic.

ridgepole A single, interior roof, support beam.

rose window A circular window with radiating tracery or glazing bars, often filled with stained glass.

rusticated masonry Masonry cut or shaped so as to create a bold, textured look, often by having beveled edges that form deep-set joints while the central face is left rough-hewn or carved with various pointed or channeled patterns.

saddle notch A saddle-shaped depression.

sanctum The enclosed part of a temple.

sash The framework or mullion that holds the glass in a window.

segmental arch One composed of less than half a circle, used over windows and doorways as an ornament.

FROM TOP: *Quoins on a street corner; a rib vault; a rose window; and a portico with rusticated masonry.*

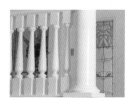

shrine A place of worship hallowed by association with some sacred thing or person.

sidelights Narrow windows flanking a doorway.

siding Boards, shingles, or other material used to surface a frame building.

sill plates Long, horizontal timbers laid on the foundation to carry the floor joists and support the posts and studs.

size Any of several gelatinous or glutinous substances, usually made from glue, wax, or clay and used as a glaze or filler for wall surfaces.

soffit The underside of a structural component—e.g., of eaves, beams, and arches.

span The length of a bridge from the beginning to the end of the structure.

spindle A wooden decoration shaped like a round stick or pin with tapered ends. Often used repeatedly to form a balustrade.

spire The slender, sharply pointed summit of a tower or roof.

stepped gable One constructed with a series of steps or curves along the roof slope, but independent of it.

stereobate *See* stylobate.

stickwork Exterior, patterned woodwork that serves an ornamental, rather than a structural, purpose; widely used on Victorian-style houses.

string course A protruding, horizontal band along the facade of a building, used to define the story levels; also called belt course.

stucco A durable finish for exterior walls, usually composed of cement, sand, and lime.

stud One of a series of vertical, wood or metal structural members in a wall frame.

stupa A funerary or commemorative mound, usually hemispherical, often containing a relic.

stylobate The immediate foundation of a row of Classical columns. Also called stereobate.

swag An ornamental drapery or curtain draped in a curve between two points, or a carving or plaster molding of such an ornament.

From top: *Sidelights;
painted spindles in a
balustrade; a stepped gable;
unpainted stucco; stupas;
and a plaster swag.*

tab A wedge-shaped stone or brick used to form ornamental patterns in masonry facades.

tapestry brick Colored brick interspersed with light-tan brick.

tenon Projecting part cut into a piece of wood for insertion into a corresponding hole (mortise) in another piece.

tented roof Roughly conical-shaped roof, built to prevent accumulations of heavy snow.

terrace A raised foundation with sloping sides; a paved, unroofed area that opens out from a building, usually at upper-story levels; a style of housing where identical, individual houses are cojoined into rows.

terra-cotta A hard, semifired ceramic clay used in pottery and building construction.

textile blocks Precast concrete blocks—often molded, with decoration on both sides or inset with glass—that can be bound together on site with steel rods and poured concrete.

tracery The branching, ornamental stone- or wood-work commonly used in Gothic-style windows to support the glass.

transept The section of a cruciform church that crosses at right angles to the greatest length between the nave and the sanctuary, or chancel.

transom A horizontal opening over a doorway that admits light and air.

trefoil A three-lobed, clover-leaf pattern.

triglyph An ornament in a Doric frieze, consisting of a projecting block having on its face two parallel vertical grooves and two half-grooves on either vertical end, that separates the metopes.

trunnel A wooden peg used to join two pieces of timber.

truss A bracket.

Tudor arch A shallow, pointed arch seen in late-medieval English architecture.

tympanum Recessed space enclosed by the slanting cornices of a pediment; also, semicircular space enclosed by an arch over the top of a door.

FROM TOP: *Terra-cotta roof tiles; tracery; a transom; a trefoil window in a gable end; and triglyphs.*

FROM TOP: *Plywood formed from glued strips of veneer; a raised verandah; vigas; a volute; a wattle-and-daub hut; and a witch's cap roof.*

valence Fabric arranged in vertical folds hung from a cornice above a window.

vault The covering over an arched area; various shapes include the semicircular or barrel vault of Romanesque architecture and the Gothic fan vault, in a concave, conical shape.

veneer A very thin layer of wood or other material for facing or inlaying wood; also, thin layers of wood glued together to form plywood for building purposes.

verandah An open or enclosed gallery or room attached to the outside of a building.

vigas The rough-hewn timber roof supports projecting from the upper facade of Pueblo-style and Hispanic buildings.

vihara Living accommodation for Buddhist monks.

volute A spiral, scroll-like ornament such as that used on an Ionic capital.

voussoir A wedge-shaped stone or brick used to form ornamental patterns on facades; also called a tab.

wainscoting The woodwork that panels the lower portion of a room.

wattle Interwoven sticks or branches used for walling, fencing, and roofing.

wattle and daub A building material composed of mud, stones, and sticks, used as infill between timber framing.

whiting Powdered chalk used in making whitewash.

whitewash A mixture of lime and water, often with whiting, size, or glue added, that is used to whiten walls, fences, or other structures.

witch's cap A shingled, conical tower roof.

INDEX